DAVID A. THOMAS

MATH PROJECTS IN THE COMPUTER AGE

PROJECTS FOR YOUNG SCIENTISTS
FRANKLIN WATTS
NEW YORK/CHICAGO/LONDON/TORONTO/SYDNEY

TO ALEXEI AND JANA

Photographs copyright ©: National Center for Supercomputing
Applications, University of Illinois at Urbana-Champaign: pp. 10, 15,
48, 105, 114; NASA: pp. 13, 54, 119, 125; Silicon Graphics, Inc./Created
by Daryl Hepting: pp. 18, 30, 47, 76, 86; Westinghouse Electric Corp.:
p. 23; National Building Museum, Washington, D.C.: p. 62; The Walt
Disney Company: p. 84; all other photos courtesy of the author.

Library of Congress Cataloging-in-Publication Data

Thomas, David A. (David Allen), 1946–
    Math projects in the computer age / David A. Thomas.
      p. cm.—(Projects for young scientists)
    Includes bibliographical references and index.
    ISBN 0-531-11213-6
      1. Mathematics—Data processing—Juvenile literature.
    2. Mathematics—Study and teaching (Secondary)—Juvenile literature.
    3. Project method in education—Juvenile literature.
    (1. Mathematics—Computer programs. 2. Programming (Computers))
    I. Title. II. Series
    QA76.95.T49   1995
    510'.78—dc20   94-42037
                                                                      CIP AC

ACKNOWLEDGMENTS

There are several people I would like to thank for supporting and contributing to the writing of this book:

• MSU graduate students Kate Riley and Tod Shockey, for their careful work in the library;

• Alexei Semenov, for his many helpful suggestions, for hosting my visit to Moscow, and for introducing me to so many talented Russian mathematicians;

• Sergei Lando and Alexander Kulakov, for many excellent project ideas; and their wives, Lena and Marina, for inviting me and my family to their homes in Moscow;

• Jana Ryslinkova, for her encouragement and for sharing the drama and commitment of her life as a Czech mathematician and educational reformer;

• John Drumheller, Dean of the College of Letters and Science at Montana State University, for his encouragement.

ABOUT THE
COMPUTER GRAPHICS

The cover is a computer simulation of a severe storm by Robert Wilhelmson and others at the National Center for Supercomputing Applications at the University of Illinois at Urbana-Champaign. The orange circles are rising particles, and the blue circles are sinking particles.

The computer graphics at the start of each chapter were generated on supercomputers and personal computers. They came from three sources:

• Daryl Hepting, a researcher at Simon Fraser University in Burnaby, British Columbia, created the opening images of Chapters 2, 3, 6, 7 on a supercomputer using iterated function systems. He and Allan Snider also generated the fern on p. 47.

• Graphics for the following chapters were generated on supercomputers at the National Center for Supercomputing Applications:

Chapters 1, 4—by Brian Evans using a fractal-based process.

Chapter 8—by Michael Norman and others, simulating an extragalactic jet passing through a shock wave.

• The author generated the friezes opening Chapter 5 and the modulus image opening Chapter 9 on a Macintosh computer.

Quark Xpress on the Macintosh platform was used for page makeup. Text typeface is Avant Garde 10 point on 13 point lead. The program Fontographer was used to create the large braces for the matrices. Most figures were redrawn with Adobe Illustrator.

CONTENTS

1

INTRODUCTION

Once in a while something really great happens in school. It can also happen at home, at the library, in a laboratory, or on a field trip. It could happen to you tonight while you're doing your homework, sitting at a computer, or thinking about a question or problem in this book. And it doesn't matter whether you are a boy or a girl. Just when you least expect it, you could discover that you are a mathematician. As unlikely as that might seem, it is a real possibility, especially if you like mathematics.

Surely, you've been surprised before. Do you remember the day you discovered you had chicken pox? All those red spots! You knew right away what that meant, didn't you? What you probably didn't realize is that you were infected with the disease many days before the symptoms appeared. You just didn't know it. Mathematical talent is often like that, unnoticed by both the student and the teachers.

This book will introduce you to a wide variety of mathematical ideas and puzzles. Treat them as candy for the mind, savoring each for its own unique qualities. Play with the ideas. Don't rush to find solutions. Let your imagination take flight as you explore the mathematical and scientific implications of the concepts, procedures, and technologies I introduce. And if it turns out that you enjoy yourself, then you are already a mathematician at heart!

PROFESSIONAL MATHEMATICIANS

A mathematician is someone who likes to think about mathematics and who uses mathematics to solve interesting problems. For instance, professional mathematicians:

- analyze the turbulent flow of air over airplane wings and around the contours of racing cars;
- make and crack secret codes;
- find ways to prevent and control unwanted vibrations in large, complex structures such as bridges, buildings, and space stations;
- compute the probability and statistics of epidemics, extinction, and global warming;
- devise strategies for winning games and optimizing the success of business ventures;
- deduce the possible geometries of other universes;
- analyze number patterns;
- study fractals, and many more topics.

Mathematicians do their work in a variety of settings. Some work in colleges and universities, splitting their time between teaching and research. Others work for the government or in business. But regardless of the setting, most mathematicians have "good" jobs.

In fact, the 1992 edition of the *Jobs Rated Almanac* included three mathematical careers—actuary, mathematician, and accountant—in its list of the ten best careers in America, based on salary, stress, work environment, outlook, security, and physical demands. (See list on p. 14.)

Four math-related careers also appear on the list: software engineer, computer systems analyst, computer pro-

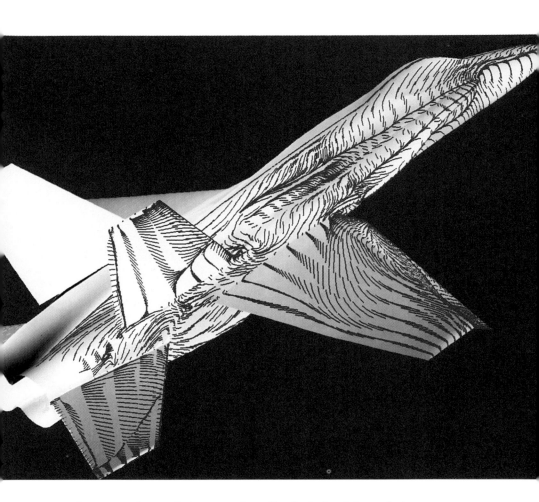

Some mathematicians analyze the turbulent flow of air over aircraft. This computer simulation shows the result of calculations on an F-18 aircraft, with airflow in red.

grammer, and meteorologist. Thus, overall, seven of the ten best careers in America are either mathematical or math-related. So, if you like math, there are good practical reasons for considering a career in mathematics or a math-related field.

STUDENT MATHEMATICIANS

If you find certain mathematical topics interesting, that's a good sign you could be a mathematician. However, it is not necessary that you find all of school mathematics interesting. In fact, that might be a bad sign since much of school mathematics is tedious and boring. A better test is whether you like mathematical puzzles. For example, do you enjoy mathematical toys like Rubik's Cube and the Tower of Hanoi? Do you enjoy games that reward logical reasoning like chess and Othello? If your school math text includes "brain teaser" puzzles, do you solve them for your own amusement? If you answered yes to any of these questions, then read on. This book was written for you!

As a student mathematician, you must strive to develop the basic skills taught in arithmetic, algebra, geometry, trigonometry, calculus, linear algebra, and other conventional mathematics courses at the high school and college levels. You will need these and other skills as a professional mathematician, scientist, or engineer. However, the purpose

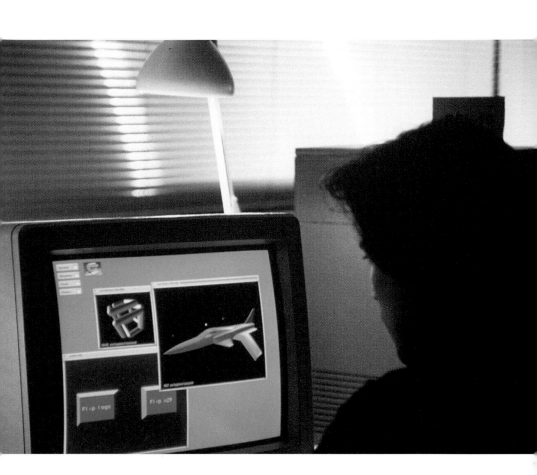

A student learns to use a computer program that analyzes the design of a jet.

of a mathematics education is not limited to skill development.

In life, nobody will hire you to work exercises out of a school mathematics book. And if you were to ask for such a job, you would be thought quite simpleminded. The real purpose of a mathematics education should be to prepare you to solve the kinds of problems that almost never appear in traditional mathematics textbooks. Realizing this fact, school officials across the country are beginning to shift the emphasis in mathematics curricula from skill development to solving non-routine problems.

One of the most useful tools for solving such problems is the computer. This book will introduce you to some simple, inexpensive computer programs that can help tremendously in completing many of the projects. If you have access to a computer, take advantage of it—the things it can do will amaze you.

This book is full of the kind of non-routine problems that have recently been recommended by the National Council of Teachers of Mathematics (NCTM), a professional organization of teachers, school administrators, and college professors. NCTM standards also call for introducing all high school students to mathematical structures such as matrices and finite graphs. Several chapters are dedicated to these topics and their applications. Other chapters address different standards.

Each chapter will introduce you to a different area of mathematics, outline several potential research projects, and suggest helpful library and computer resources. The prior knowledge required for the projects varies. Any middle school or high school student should be able to find a project to match his or her mathematics interests. The number theory projects in Chapter 9, for example, require little or no prior knowledge. Even if you are not yet ready to tackle a particular project, the project description will at least show you the extraordinary feats mathematics makes possible; hopefully, that will inspire you to learn more mathematics.

If you choose to do an independent research project from this book, you are advancing your mathematics education in precisely the direction it should go. Regardless of the topic you choose, you will inevitably address the four standards considered most important by the NCTM:

• Mathematics as Problem Solving—you will apply what

you already know about mathematics to solve your research problem;

    • Mathematics as Communication—you will talk with an adviser and mentor, write a final report, and present your findings to other students and teachers;

    • Mathematics as Reasoning—you will make and test conjectures and judge the validity of various arguments; and

    • Mathematical Connections—you will explore the relationships between your research problem and similar problems in other branches of mathematics and/or science.

As you engage in these activities, you will develop the skills, attitudes, and habits of a real mathematician. Welcome to the club!

2

THE STUDENT PROJECT

Students do mathematics research projects for a variety of reasons. Many are done as term projects for a particular course. For example, your geometry teacher might ask you to write a report describing the uses of geodesic domes in architecture. This type of research is basically historical in nature and requires the student to play the role of an observer or reporter rather than a participant. By that, I mean that the research task does not include the expectation that the student will develop new mathematical insights, formulas, or models, but rather will report on what others have discovered. This type of research requires good library and writing skills and is typically accomplished in a few days' time.

If a project is to be competitive in a science fair or science talent search, it must go beyond historical reporting. For a project on geodesic domes, a computer program might be developed to design domes to various specifications. A final report for such a project should include historical information, demonstrate mastery of the basic mathematics concepts and skills associated with geodesic dome design, and highlight the researcher's creative insights.

Projects of this sort are also carried out by students attending summer institutes at colleges and universities. They must have all of the skills needed for historical research, a genuine interest in mathematics, and a commitment to participate personally in the process called discovery. This type of research is rarely accomplished in a short period and may extend over several months.

The projects in this book are of the second sort. It is therefore important that you choose your topic carefully, for you will live with it for many weeks.

GETTING STARTED

As a novice mathematics researcher, you should ideally work under the direction of an adviser at school and possibly a mentor at a local college or university. These people will make your research project more meaningful and more fun. Begin by talking to your mathematics teacher. Explain that you would like to do a research project and ask whether he or she can help you find someone to act as your local adviser.

The most important role of this adviser is to help you choose a suitable project and to assist you in your search for further information and expert mathematical assistance. Your adviser may also arrange for you to meet informally from week to week with other student researchers at your school. Talking about your project and listening to other students do the same are important aspects of mathematical research. They can also be fun!

Once you have settled on a topic and have an adviser at your school, you should look for a research supervisor, commonly called a mentor. A mentor is an experienced mathematician who is willing to help you with the details of your research, particularly when you "get stuck." Your mentor may be your adviser, another teacher at school, a teacher at another school, or a professor at a local college or university.

If your adviser is not your mentor, he or she may know of someone in your town who has the necessary expertise. If that is the case, ask your adviser to arrange a meeting, perhaps at your school or at the proposed mentor's office. Your parents may also want to attend the meeting. If your proposed mentor is in another town at a college or university, a day trip should be planned that will give you an opportunity to visit with your mentor, tour the school's library and computer facilities, meet with other faculty members, and so on. All this can be very exciting. Just be sure to get everyone's address, phone number, fax number, and electronic mail (e-mail) address. You should also give your mentor your address and phone numbers at home and at school.

If your mentor is in another town, you may find yourself communicating with her or with him by mail, phone, fax, or e-mail. Because this correspondence is an important part of the research process, be sure to keep good notes on what you send to and receive from your mentor.

All of this correspondence, along with your other research notes, should be organized in a file or research notebook. If you enter your project in a science fair or similar competition, you may be required to produce such a notebook. It is far better to organize your materials from the start and maintain a good set of records than to try to reconstruct what happened after the fact.

In addition to the help you receive from your adviser and mentor, you may also wish to consult other experts. Appendix A at the end of the book lists the addresses of the various state offices of public education. In most of these offices, there is a mathematics education specialist who may be able to give you the names and phone numbers of additional contacts. Appendix B contains the names and addresses of a number of professional organizations that have an interest in mathematics education. A letter to these organizations may also lead to valuable assistance.

EXAMPLES OF STUDENT RESEARCH

Frequently, students begin mathematics research projects with a specific goal in mind, such as entering them in a science fair or science talent search competition. These competitions are organized at the school, school district, state, regional, and national levels by a variety of sponsoring organizations. At the national level, the two best known competitions are the International Science and Engineering Fair and the Westinghouse Science Talent Search. Every year, thousands of students enter these competitions, gaining valuable experience and occasionally winning scholarships and other prizes.

The Westinghouse Science Talent Search is a national competition open to high school seniors. Since 1942, this annual event has sought to identify and reward young scientific talent. Every December participants mail their entries to Science Service (1719 N Street NW, Washington, DC 20036; phone: 202-785-2255). Each entry consists of an official Westinghouse Science Talent Search entry form and a written report documenting a student research project.

A distinguished board of judges reviews all entries and chooses 300 for honors awards. From this honors group, 40 contestants are named to the winners group. These 40 students receive all-expense-paid trips to Washington, DC, for the final judging and awards ceremony, where $140,000 in scholarships is given away.

Throughout the history of the Science Talent Search, students submitting mathematics projects have fared well in competition with students entering projects in microbiology, biology, chemistry, earth science, physics, and other scientific disciplines. The following list of winners and honors mathematics projects should reassure both teachers and students that research opportunities abound and that judges look

**Robert Christopher Sarvis placed fourth in the 1994
Westinghouse Science Talent search with his math project
on trees—graphs with no loops—in lattices. His topic has
application in microchip design, fractal geometry,
chemistry, and the study of crystal growth.**

favorably on mathematics research. If the topics sound over-
whelming to you now, don't be discouraged; the projects
were carried out by students just like you!

Winners Math Projects

• An Investigation of Trees in Lattices: Robert Christopher
Sarvis studied a specifically defined tree, which is a graph
with no loops, in certain lattices (1994).

• Applications of Minkowski's Theorem to Classical

Number Theory: Moon Duchin used Minkowski's First Lattice Point Theorem to prove many theorems from classical number theory, using geometric arguments that were much shorter than conventional algebraic proofs (1993).

- Closer to Being Equilateral: Jared Ian Muroff investigated a new method of proving triangle inequalities (1990).
- Derivation of the Pythagorean Theorem: Simple Harmonic Motion and Pythagorean Triples Revisited: Corey Cheng developed a new proof of the Pythagorean theorem and investigated its implications in a variety of mathematical and physical contexts (1990).
- Grocery-Shopping Problem and Extensions: Lenhard Lee Ng studied the probability that a shopper would accurately estimate the total cost of a number of groceries to the nearest dollar by rounding each item's price to the nearest dollar (1993).
- Hysteresis and the Structure of Fractal Basin Boundaries in the Henon System: Using a computer model that he created to investigate the Henon dynamical system, David D. Ben-Zvi discovered and proved a new theorem (1990).
- Investigation of Generalized Sigma Function Over Certain Metric Spaces: Andrew Olstrom Dittmer investigated whether there are any odd perfect numbers (1993).
- Investigation of k-ary n-tuples of Integers: Jordan S. Ellenberg studied sets of positive integers satisfying certain symmetric systems of congruence (1989).
- Matching Two Curves by Transformation of Two Piecewise Developable Surfaces: Royce Yung-Tze Peng investigated whether two planar curves, each with a smooth edge on its boundary, could be bent without stretching and joined at the edges (1990).
- Methods for Solution of Permutation Equations: Simon Robert Zuckerbraun discovered a new class of problems while playing with a Rubik's Cube and developed methods for solving them (1989).
- Multi-Dimensional Extension of Wythoff's Game: Steve

Shaw-Tang Chien extended the rules for Wythoff's Game to higher dimensions and devised a winning strategy (1993).

• Numerical Solutions of Minimal Surfaces: Andrew Matthew Lines' computer program can predict the shape of a soap film produced when a wire frame is dipped into soapy water (1990).

• On the Diophantine Equation $ap^x + bq^y = c + dp^zq^w$: Christopher McLean Skinner investigated a form of Diophantine equation and demonstrated the existence of an upper bound on the integral solutions of certain equations (1989).

• On Constructing Polygons on Orthogonal Integral Lattices: Shinpei Kuga developed two mathematical proofs involving the construction of polygons drawn with their vertices on points having integral coordinates (1990).

• On Solving Fractions Represented by p-adic Integers: Ahuangzhuang (Alex) Peng created a computer program to investigate the integers used to represent fractions under a modulus of a power of a prime (1992).

• On Highly Composite Numbers: Igor Yakovlevich Tsukerman investigated highly composite numbers using a computer program that he wrote (1992).

• On the Diophantine Equation $x^m + D = g^n$: Mahesh Kalyana Mahanthappa developed a method for finding integer solutions to the general exponential Diophantine equation (1993).

• p-adic Continued Fractions: Joshua Bailey Fischman developed a computer program to investigate continued fractions in a number system based on prime numbers (1990).

• Representing Integers in the Quadratic Ring of Z(square root of -2) as a Sum of Two Z(square root of -2) Squares: Put Cheung investigated the problem of representing integers as the sum of squares in an algebraic structure known as Z(square root of -2) (1990).

• Solving Pell's Equation in Gaussian Integers: Michail

Leyb Sunitsky developed solutions to the equation $x^2 - dy^2 = \pm 1$ in Gaussian integers (1992).

- The Peg Solitaire Army: Wei-Hwa Huang modified the puzzle game "Peg Solitaire" and investigated winning strategies (1993).
- Traversal Problems for Certain Types of Deterministic and Non-Deterministic Automata: Leonid Ntanovich Reyzin investigated problems encountered by two types of robots attempting to traverse geometrical structures (1992).
- Trinomial Fermat Numbers: Wai Ling Ma defined a new type of number and investigated its properties (1989).

Honors Math Projects
- A Universal 416-State 9-Neighbor Cellular Automaton.
- A Disproof of Identical Vanishment for the Riemann Christoffel Curvature and the Ricci Curvature Invariant.
- A Parallel Algorithm for Newton's Method Convergence for Complex Functions with Rational Exponents.
- Algebraic Analysis of Continued Fractions in a Polynomial Ring.
- Algebraic and Geometric Analysis of Continued Fractions in the Ring of Eisenstein Integers.
- Almost All Boolean Functions Are Strongly Non-Monotone.
- Alpha-Abundant Numbers.
- Approximating $y = 2^{x-1}$ by Polynomials Derived from Pascal's Triangle.
- Bi-unitary Hyperperfect Numbers.
- Brownian Motion: The Statistical Analysis of the Position Distribution.
- Controlling Fractal Growth in Dynamic Environment Using Adaptive Non-Deterministic Attractors.
- Can Perfect Numbers Be Odd?
- Chaotic Analysis Technique for the Planar Restricted Three-Body Problem.

- Communications Efficiency as Extremal Problem in Graph Theory.
- Computational Dynamics of Mass Transfer Binary Star System.
- Computer Assisted Space Mapping.
- Continuous Solutions of the Functional Equation $g(x - y) = g(x)g(y) + f(x)f(y)$.
- Decimal Fractions with Connections to Divisibility Rules and Cyclic Numbers.
- Defective Coloring of Graphs in Surfaces with "m" Colors.
- Determining the Characteristics of "Neglected" Number Theory Functions $sigma(n)/n$ and $s(n)/n$.
- Determining Whether a Rational Integer Is a Quadratic Residue of Another Rational Integer, Extended and Generalized to the Ring of Gaussian Integers, $Z(i)$.
- Determining the Dimension of Fractals Generated by Pascal's Triangle.
- Dynamical and Statistical Study of Chaos in a One-Dimensional Self-Gravitating System.
- Dynamics of Circle Maps and the One-Way Property.
- Effectiveness of Various Priority Queing Algorithms as Applied to a Multitasking System.
- Examining the Theory of Self-Similarity in Phase Diagrams of Stock Market Data.
- Examining a New Function.
- Experimental Turbulence and the k-Epsilon Transport Equations.
- Exploring Number Theory with Finite State Automation.
- Extensive Study of P_t-Sets.
- The Fixed Ratio Among the Sides of Two Congruent Rectangles' Overlap Area.
- Formalized Method for Finding the Symmetry Operations Matrices of Point Groups of Known Coordinates and Its Application in the Simplification of the Force Constant Matrix of the Icosahedral Buckyball Molecule.

- Formula Representation for the Summation of k^p.
- Fractal Galaxy Distribution in the Evolving Universe.
- Fractal Dimensional Analysis of Non-Flagellated Bacterial Colonies.
- Fractal Dimension of Turbulence.
- Fractals: A New Measurement for Sunspots.
- Frequency-Modulation Waveform Approximations.
- Fuzzy Logic and Bayesian Belief Networks Applied to Passive Sonar Automatic Detection and Tracking.
- Generalization of Theorems Concerning the Sums of Squares of Integers and Gaussian Integers to the Quaternions.
- Higher Order Pascal's Triangles and Their Applications to Extensions of a Child's Game.
- Implementing Infinite Precision Computer Arithmetic for Real Numbers Using the C++ Language.
- Mathematical Simulation of Lightning Stepped Leaders.
- Mathematical and Computational Investigation of Superduperperfect Numbers.
- Mathematical and Physical Simulations of Tidal Bores.
- Mixed Continued Fractions: A New Representation of $(d)^{1/2}$.
- Monte Carlo Simulations of Photon Flight Through Diffuse Materials.
- Non-Simple Continued Fractions.
- Not-So-Perfect Numbers.
- nth Power Residues.
- Number Theoretical Analysis of Polynomials and Their Derivatives Having Integer Roots.
- On Parabolic Functions and Their Applications.
- On the Order p Reversal Equation: $Rev(n^p) = (Rev(n))^p$.
- Optimization of Sorting Time Using Non-Random Lists.
- Orthogonal Function Set in Two Variables.
- Outsmarting Chaos.
- Partial Analysis of a One-Dimensional Dynamical System.
- Preliminary Investigation of the Sigma Function in the Ring of Eisenstein Integers.

- Probabilistic Network Applied to Seismic and Reliability Problems: A New Approach.
- Proofs and Corollaries of Pascal's "Mystic Hexagram" Theorem.
- Research of P_t Sets.
- Rings of Small Order: A Computer-Aided Study.
- Some Estimation About Delauncy Graphs in Lr-Metric in E^2.
- Space-Filling Curve in the N-Dimensional Euclidean Space.
- Study of the Omega Function.
- Study of Divisors.
- Study of the Rho Function and Other Related Functions.
- Symbolically Determining the Intersection of Surfaces in Three-Space.
- The Function $Omega_2(n)$ and Multiply-Square-Perfect Numbers.
- Two Theorems from Power Residue Sequences.

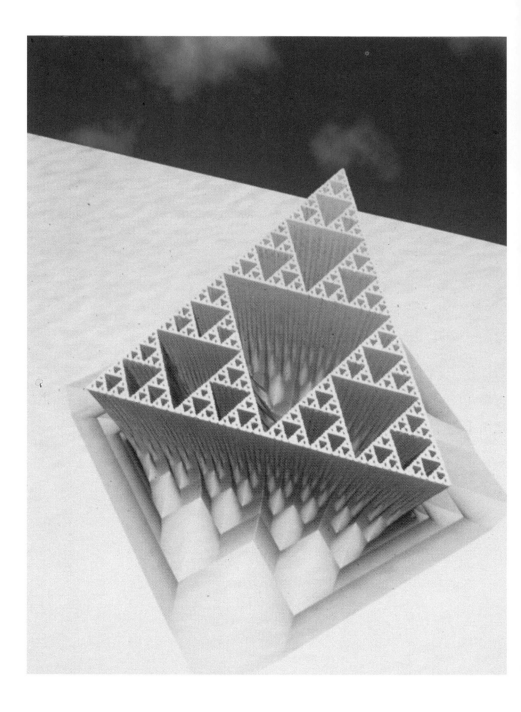

3

LINEAR ALGEBRA
AND MATRICES

Long before the nineteenth-century English mathematician Arthur Caley devised our modern system of matrix algebra, Chu Shikie wrote about matrix algebra in China in 1299 and 1303 during the time of the Yuan dynasty. Today, matrix algebra is a powerful mathematical tool for modeling complex problems and computing their solutions. Engineers use it routinely to solve systems of equations describing the flow of electrons in electrical circuits, fluids through pipes, and traffic in cities. It helps generals predict the outcome of war games. Businesses make important supply-and-demand decisions based on matrix algebra.

We'll start with a discussion of matrix algebra and its value in solving systems of linear equations. Then in this and the following three chapters, we'll discuss some exciting applications made possible by this simple tool.

SOLVING SYSTEMS OF EQUATIONS

The subject of linear equations—the equations that represent straight lines—is an important and time-consuming topic in introductory algebra. Typically, students learn to write linear equations in three forms:

Slope-intercept form	$y = mx + b$
Point-slope form	$y - y_1 = m(x - x_1)$
Standard form	$Ax + By = C$

These kinds of representation are called functional notation. Matrix notation offers a different way of representing the same thing. Equations in standard form are most easily translated to matrix notation.

In matrix notation, the equation $Ax + By = C$ is written as

$$[A \ B] \begin{bmatrix} x \\ y \end{bmatrix} = C$$

with the coefficients appearing as the row vector $[A \ B]$ and the variables as a column vector. The product of these two vectors is found by multiplying the nth element of the row vector by the corresponding nth element of the column vector and summing these products. In this case, the procedure generates the equation $Ax + By = C$.

The advantages of matrix notation become apparent when solving systems of linear equations. For example, the system

$$Ax + By = E$$
$$Cx + Dy = F$$

may be thought of as representing two straight lines. If the two lines intersect at a single point, that point must lie on both lines and therefore satisfies both equations. Points that satisfy every equation in a system of equations are called solutions of the system of equations. If the two lines do not intersect, then there is no point that satisfies both equations. In such a case, the system of equations has no solution. The third possibility is that the two equations are different representations of the same line. In this case, there are infinitely many points that satisfy both equations and therefore infinitely many solutions to the system.

Students in introductory algebra are normally taught two methods for solving systems of two or three equations. The methods are called linear combination and substitution. Although convenient for small systems of equations, these methods are tedious and time consuming when the number of equations and variables surpasses four or five. That is when matrix algebra comes in handy.

The previous system of two equations may be represented as the matrix equation

$$\begin{bmatrix} A & B \\ C & D \end{bmatrix} \begin{bmatrix} x \\ y \end{bmatrix} = \begin{bmatrix} E \\ F \end{bmatrix}$$

With this notation, it is easy to represent systems having large numbers of variables and equations. The matrix at the left, the coefficient matrix, contains a row for each equation.

It is common practice to represent the coefficient matrix for a system of equations with the letter A, the column of variables with the letter x, and the column of constants with the letter C. Using this convention, the equation above becomes $Ax = C$, which looks much friendlier. That look is deceiving, for the procedures involved in matrix multiplication are complex and tedious to do by hand for large numbers of equations.

Fortunately, computer programs that will do the work for you are widely available. My favorite is a program called MATLAB, which is short for matrix laboratory. It is described in detail in Chapter 4. My advice to student researchers is to get a clear understanding of what matrices are and how they may be manipulated to achieve different objectives; then get a copy of MATLAB or some comparable software product and do all your calculations by computer.

We now turn our attention to what the solution to a system of linear equations might mean in terms of a variety of applications. This is where things get interesting!

TRAFFIC ANALYSIS

Urban planners and civil engineers use systems of equations to describe the flow of automobile traffic through city streets. A simple example is shown in Figure 3.1. The traffic flow along the grid of one-way streets defined by A Street, B Street, 1st Avenue, and 2nd Avenue is as follows:

LOCATION	FLOW IN CARS PER HOUR	DIRECTION
1	300	East
2	800	South
3	600	North
4	400	East
5	700	West
6	200	North
7	800	South
8	200	West

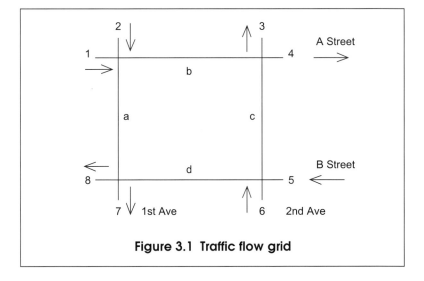

Figure 3.1 Traffic flow grid

Suppose you want to compute the traffic flows a, b, c, and d. Remembering that the flow into any intersection must equal the flow out of the intersection, we can write the following system of equations:

INTERSECTION	TRAFFIC EQUATION
A St and 1st Ave	$a + b = 300 + 800$
A St and 2nd Ave	$b + c = 600 + 400$
B St and 1st Ave	$a + d = 800 + 200$
B St and 2nd Ave	$c + d = 700 + 200$

This system simplifies to:

$$a + b = 1100$$
$$b + c = 1000$$
$$a + d = 1000$$
$$c + d = 900$$

which in matrix notation looks like:

$$\begin{bmatrix} 1 & 1 & 0 & 0 \\ 0 & 1 & 1 & 0 \\ 1 & 0 & 0 & 1 \\ 0 & 0 & 1 & 1 \end{bmatrix} \begin{bmatrix} a \\ b \\ c \\ d \end{bmatrix} = \begin{bmatrix} 1100 \\ 1000 \\ 1000 \\ 900 \end{bmatrix}$$

When this equation is solved by MATLAB, the system turns out to have infinitely many solutions, each of which consists of a related set of flows a, b, c, and d where, given any choice for d, $a = 1000 - d$, $b = 100 + d$, and $c = 900 - d$. For example, if we let $d = 500$, then $a = 500$, $b = 600$, and $c = 400$. If we let $d = 0$ (i.e., we block off the street), $a = 1000$, $b = 100$, and $c = 900$.

If the complexity of the street system increases, more and more variables and equations must be added to the system of equations. A similar approach may be taken when analyzing the flow of liquids through a water or sewage system, the flow of electrons through an electronic circuit, and many other situations. Try the following research projects:

Project 3.1

Find out whether data is kept on traffic flow patterns in your town. If a construction project is being planned that would interrupt traffic on a main street or if a parade is scheduled that would close certain streets to regular traffic, see whether you can arrange to work with the city engineer to model changes in traffic during the interruption. Then gather data on what actually happens and assess the validity of your mathematical model.

Project 3.2

An important function of local government is the management of the city's water supply. Water flow at various pumping stations and reservoirs is normally monitored quite closely. Talk to your city engineer about a project to model the local water transport system, including waste water in sewer and storm drains. Use your model and MATLAB to identify potential problems in the event that the city would have to close off specific storm drains and sewers. Prepare a report that includes the predictions of your model. If possible, compare your predictions to actual events recorded in the city records to assess the validity of your model.

LINEAR TRANSFORMATIONS OF THE EUCLIDEAN PLANE

A linear transformation may be thought of as a particular type of distortion of a plane—a distortion in which rectangles are transformed into parallelograms. In linear transformations, straight lines remain straight but angles between lines can change. Figure 3.2 shows the Euclidean plane—the coordinate system you learned in school—and a unit square before and after a linear transformation.

To calculate the new coordinates of a point after a linear transformation, you would use equations of the form $x' = ax + by + c$ and $y' = dx + ey + f$, where (x, y) is the point before transformation and (x', y') is the image of the point

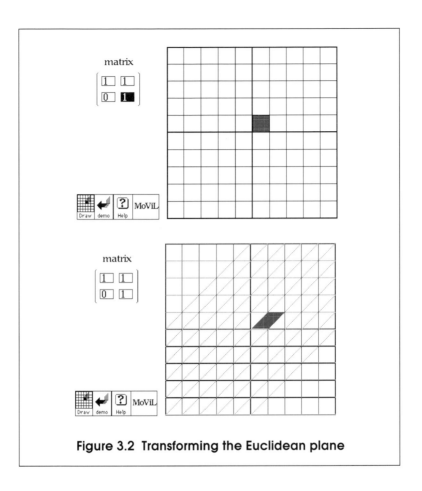

Figure 3.2 Transforming the Euclidean plane

after transformation. Thus, each new coordinate is a linear combination of the *x*- and *y*-coordinates of the original point. Visually, this means that while line segments remain straight, their length and direction may change. Parallel lines remain parallel, and lines that intersect before transformation intersect after transformation, though the angle formed by the two lines may change.

A linear transformation *T* is usually represented in functional notation as $T(x, y) = (x', y') = (ax + by + c, dx + ey + f)$.

In matrix notation, this expression may be written using a 2 x 2 matrix and a 2 x 1 translation vector as

$$\begin{bmatrix} x' \\ y' \end{bmatrix} = \begin{bmatrix} a & b \\ d & e \end{bmatrix} \begin{bmatrix} x \\ y \end{bmatrix} + \begin{bmatrix} c \\ f \end{bmatrix}$$

To simplify matters, linear transformations of the Euclidean plane may also be represented by single 3 x 3 matrices. This may be accomplished by thinking of the Euclidean plane as the plane $Z = 1$ in three-dimensional space. It is the plane parallel to and one unit above the *XY* plane. All points in this plane have a z-coordinate of 1 and are represented by (x, y, 1). This system of notation is called homogeneous coordinates. If the linear transformation *T* is applied to a point (x, y, 1) in the Euclidean plane, we represent that transformation as follows:

$$T * \begin{bmatrix} x \\ y \\ 1 \end{bmatrix} = \begin{bmatrix} x' \\ y' \\ 1 \end{bmatrix}, \text{ or } \begin{bmatrix} a & b & c \\ d & e & f \\ 0 & 0 & 1 \end{bmatrix} \begin{bmatrix} x \\ y \\ 1 \end{bmatrix} = \begin{bmatrix} x' \\ y' \\ 1 \end{bmatrix}$$

Any choice of real numbers for *a, b, c, d, e,* and *f* will result in a linear transformation *T*, as long as the determinant of *T* is not zero.

Figure 3.3 shows a unit square on an inverted coordinate system like those typically found on computer screens. The corners of the square are {(0, 0), (1, 0), (0, 1), (1, 1)}.

If a linear transformation matrix *T* defined as

$$T = \begin{bmatrix} \frac{1}{2} & 0 & \frac{7}{16} \\ 0 & \frac{1}{2} & \frac{1}{4} \\ 0 & 0 & 1 \end{bmatrix}$$

is applied to the plane, the vertical and horizontal dimensions of any object in the plane will shrink by half, in combination with a horizontal shift of $\frac{7}{16}$ and a vertical shift of $\frac{1}{4}$. In

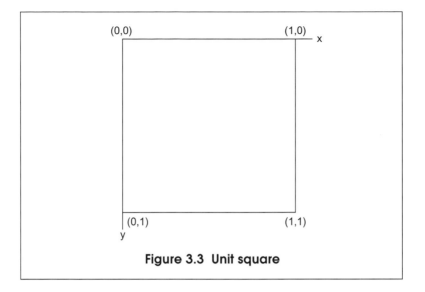

Figure 3.3 Unit square

this kind of transformation, known as a contraction mapping, all the points of the plane move closer together.

There is one point, however, that does not move at all; it is called the fixed point of the transformation. This point, (x_f, y_f), is a solution to the matrix equation

$$\begin{bmatrix} \frac{1}{2} & 0 & \frac{7}{16} \\ 0 & \frac{1}{2} & \frac{1}{4} \\ 0 & 0 & 1 \end{bmatrix} \begin{bmatrix} x \\ y \\ 1 \end{bmatrix} = \begin{bmatrix} x \\ y \\ 1 \end{bmatrix}$$

In this case, the fixed point is $(\frac{7}{8}, \frac{1}{2})$. And, since the transformation is a contraction mapping, every point on the plane moves closer to the fixed point with successive applications of T. For this reason, fixed points of this sort are called attractors. If you make a mental movie of this process, you should imagine the entire plane being drawn into the attractor as if the fixed point were a kind of mathematical black hole.

From considering one linear transformation and its fixed

point, we now move on to consider a system of three linear transformations $\{T_1, T_2, T_3\}$ where

$$T_1 = \begin{bmatrix} \frac{1}{2} & 0 & 0 \\ 0 & \frac{1}{2} & 0 \\ 0 & 0 & 1 \end{bmatrix} \quad T_2 = \begin{bmatrix} \frac{1}{2} & 0 & \frac{1}{2} \\ 0 & \frac{1}{2} & 0 \\ 0 & 0 & 1 \end{bmatrix} \quad T_3 = \begin{bmatrix} \frac{1}{2} & 0 & \frac{1}{4} \\ 0 & \frac{1}{2} & \frac{1}{2} \\ 0 & 0 & 1 \end{bmatrix}$$

Each of these transformations is a contraction mapping with x-scale and y-scale factors of $\frac{1}{2}$, but with different fixed points. They are $(0, 0)$, $(1, 0)$, and $(\frac{1}{2}, 1)$, respectively.

Each transformation would map the starting unit square to a smaller square as shown in Figure 3.4. In the first transformation, the unit square is mapped to the shaded region marked T_1.

Similarly, the second and third transformations would map to regions T_2 and T_3. Note that no region of the original unit square would be mapped to the unshaded part of Figure 3.4. It should also be clear that the shaded regions occupy $\frac{3}{4}$ of the original area of the unit square. To put it simply, these

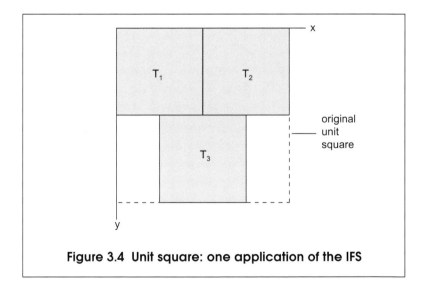

Figure 3.4 Unit square: one application of the IFS

shaded regions show where a point in the original unit square might end up after one transformation.

Now consider a sequence of two transformations, T_i and T_j: Where might the image of a point in the original unit square end up after it undergoes two successive mappings? Figure 3.5 shows nine shaded regions, each representing a different pair of the transformations we considered previously. Since there are nine regions, you may surmise that matrix multiplication is typically not commutative; that is, you get a different answer depending on the order of the matrices. Note also that the shaded region now occupies only $\frac{9}{16}$ of the original unit square.

Going a step further, Figure 3.6 shows the result of applying three successive transformations to the unit square. Applying all possible sequences of the three transformations produces 27 regions where an image point may be found, an area constituting $\frac{27}{64}$ of the unit square.

What happens as we apply more and more transformations? In general, after n transformations, the shaded area

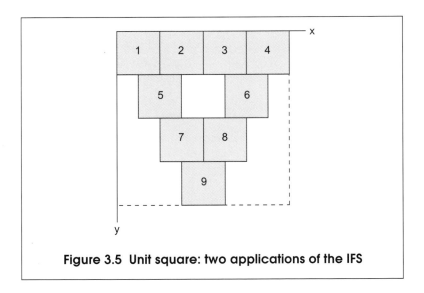

Figure 3.5 Unit square: two applications of the IFS

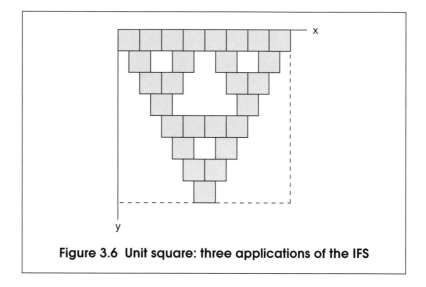

Figure 3.6 Unit square: three applications of the IFS

will consist of 3^n regions occupying $\left(\frac{3}{4}\right)^n$ of the unit square. As n approaches infinity, the number of regions approaches infinity while the area occupied by those regions approaches zero. The theoretical object that emerges as n goes to infinity is an exquisitely detailed set of points called the Sierpinski gasket. Figure 3.7 shows the general form of this object.

The Sierpinski gasket is an example of a self-similar object called a fractal, in which a feature is repeated over and over again at different magnifications. What is most astonishing about the previous exercise is that a system of three linear equations, each having a fixed-point attractor, ends up generating an attractor with an infinite number of points. Indeed, the Sierpinski gasket is called a "strange" attractor because the result is so unexpected and odd. Even more astonishing, there is a very simple procedure for generating an approximation of the strange attractor in such systems. Michael Barnsley calls it "the chaos game" in his 1988 book *Fractals Everywhere.*

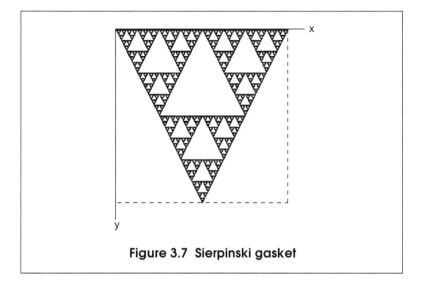

Figure 3.7 Sierpinski gasket

Given any system of contractive linear transformations, the chaos game proceeds as follows. Select a "seed point" at random in the plane. Apply any one of the linear transformations, and determine the location of the seed point's image. Input the coordinates of this point into a second randomly selected linear transformation. Repeat the process thousands of times on a computer, and a set of several thousand points will be generated on the computer screen.

It is a simple matter to write a BASIC program to mimic this process. One such program is the following:

```
10      SCREEN 1
20      X = 0: Y = 0
30      I = INT(4*RND(1)+1)
40      IF I = 1 THEN WX = .6*X + .18: WY = .6*Y + .35
50      IF I = 2 THEN WX = .6*X + .18: WY = .6*Y + .12
60      IF I = 3 THEN WX = .4*X + .3*Y + .27: WY = −.3*X +
        .4*Y + .36
```

```
70      IF I = 4 THEN WX = .4*X – .3*Y + .27: WY = .3*X +
        .4*Y + .09
80      X = WX: Y = WY
90      PX = INT(X*250): PY = INT((1 – Y)*250)
100     PSET (PX,PY)
110     GOTO 30
```

If you run the program, you will get an object that looks like a Christmas tree, as shown in Figure 3.8.

Surprisingly, no matter how many times you run the chaos game for a particular system, the images always look the same, even though the random selection of transformations leads to a different set of points for each image. The explanation for this astonishing result is that the images are approximations of the same theoretical entity—the strange attractor

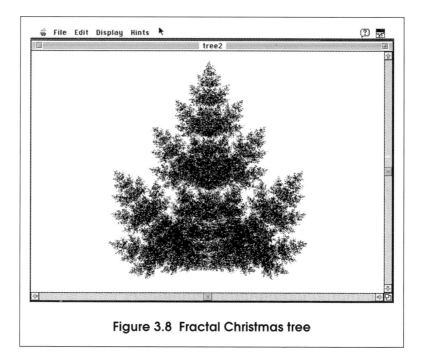

Figure 3.8 Fractal Christmas tree

of an iterated function system (IFS). (An IFS refers to any series of functions that are applied in succession to an object.) How can this be? It's like pea plants all grown from the same pod of seeds. They may differ in a few details, but given basically the same sun, water, and soil, they will turn out to be remarkably similar. The strange attractor of an IFS corresponds to the pea plant you'd get if it had the ideal amount of sun and water and a perfect soil in which to grow.

In the chaos game, we have a mathematical metaphor for growth in the natural world. For example, you might be considered an approximation of the strange attractor determined by your DNA! Every day of your life, your cells repeat the same set of operations. Sure, if you'd had more vitamins, you might have grown taller. And if you'd never had that childhood disease you might have been stronger. But you would still be *you*, only healthier.

You may be able to guess a few of the broad features of an attractor before it is created, but you can never know the specific points that will be produced along the way. The unpredictable nature of the random process used to generate the points guarantees that you can never know the final result without actually going through all the intermediate steps. To an observer, the process is chaotic even though the result is ordered.

Here, then, is an aspect of mathematics for which computer visualization is indispensable.

Students can define IFS systems, run them on a computer, and watch the strange attractors materialize on the screen. With a little practice, you can design strange attractors to have specific characteristics. Two particularly helpful software packages for this type of work are The Desktop Fractal Design System and Chaos: The Software.

In designing linear transformations for IFS systems, the only condition is that each transformation must be a contraction mapping; that is, the transformation must move points closer together rather than farther apart. Applying this condition to the transformation matrix

$$\begin{bmatrix} a & b & c \\ d & e & f \\ 0 & 0 & 1 \end{bmatrix}$$

is part of Project 3.3.

Project 3.3
Which choices of matrix entries a–f produce linear transformations that are
- translations of the plane;
- rotations of the plane about a fixed point;
- reflections of the plane along a fixed line;
- similarity transformations—that is, simple enlargements or reductions;
- skew transformations, such as changing a square to a parallelogram;
- strain transformations—expanding or compressing in one dimension;
- contraction mappings?

Project 3.4
Every linear transformation is uniquely determined by any three non-collinear (non-aligned) points and their images under the transformation. In other words, there is only one linear transformation that would move all three points to the image points. Develop a procedure for finding any linear transformation, given such sets of points.

Project 3.5
In the computer language of your choice (BASIC, PASCAL, or C), write a chaos game program for generating strange attractors. Begin with the linear transformations T_1, T_2, and T_3 given previously. Then modify the transformations and add more transformations to generate a variety of strange attractors. What relationships can you discover between the overall appearances of strange attractors and the individual linear transformations on which they are based?

**Iterated function systems can create objects
that resemble flora such as ferns.**

Project 3.6
Create IFSs that have strange attractors resembling objects
from nature, such as ferns, leaves, and weeds. Explore the
applications of IFSs in other disciplines such as geology or
physics.

4

BASIC COMPUTER TOOLS

In recent years computers have become integral to mathematicians' research activities. For many student researchers, one of the most exciting benefits of doing a math research project is learning to use powerful computational and visualization tools. This chapter covers several inexpensive (or free) computer tools that can help you with your projects. They can take care of all the tedious computation for you.

MATLAB AND LINEAR ALGEBRA

MATLAB is a user-friendly matrix algebra program for IBM-compatible microcomputers. Originally developed by Cleve B. Moler in 1984 at the University of New Mexico under a National Science Foundation grant, MATLAB offers students a convenient tool for solving matrix algebra problems. Readers may obtain a copy of MATLAB on 5.25- or 3.5-inch disks for $5 from Public Brand Software (phone 1-800-426-DISK). A basic instruction manual can be printed from the disk. As a resource for interesting problems and MATLAB applications, readers should consider getting the 1988 book *Experiments in Computational Matrix Algebra* by David R. Hill.

MATLAB COMMANDS

Creating matrices and operating on them are easy in MAT-LAB. The following examples will give you an idea of what MATLAB can do.

1. To define a 3 x 3 matrix A, type
   A = <1 1 1;2 3 1;1 2 1>
   and MATLAB responds

   $$A = \begin{bmatrix} 1 & 1 & 1 \\ 2 & 3 & 1 \\ 1 & 2 & 1 \end{bmatrix}$$

2. To find the transpose of A, type
   A′
   and MATLAB responds

   $$ans = \begin{bmatrix} 1 & 2 & 1 \\ 1 & 3 & 2 \\ 1 & 1 & 1 \end{bmatrix}$$

3. Matrices may also be easily added, subtracted, multiplied, or raised to powers. For example, if C and D are square matrices of the same size, the following commands are legal:
   Addition: C+D
   Subtraction: C−D
   Multiplication: C*D
   Raise C to the 4th power: C**4

4. To find the inverse of A, type
   inv(A)
   and MATLAB responds

$$\text{ans} = \begin{bmatrix} 1 & 1 & -2 \\ -1 & 0 & 1 \\ 1 & -1 & 1 \end{bmatrix}$$

5. To find the determinant of A, type
   det(A)
   and MATLAB responds
   ans =1

6. MATLAB also easily solves systems of equations. For example, suppose that a system of three equations in three unknowns is represented by $Ax = b$, where

$$A = \begin{bmatrix} 3 & 4 & -1 \\ 1 & -2 & 2 \\ -1 & 0 & 1 \end{bmatrix} \quad x = \begin{bmatrix} x_1 \\ x_2 \\ x_3 \end{bmatrix} \quad \text{and } b = \begin{bmatrix} 8 \\ 3 \\ 2 \end{bmatrix}$$

   These matrices may be created with the following MATLAB commands:
   A = <3 4 -1;1 -2 2;-1 0 1>
   b = <8;3;2>
   MATLAB responds with

$$A = \begin{bmatrix} 3 & 4 & -1 \\ 1 & -2 & 2 \\ -1 & 0 & 1 \end{bmatrix}$$

$$b = \begin{bmatrix} 8 \\ 3 \\ 2 \end{bmatrix}$$

To solve the equation, simply type
A/b
MATLAB gives the solution as *xcomp*:

$$\text{xcomp} = \begin{bmatrix} 1 \\ 2 \\ 3 \end{bmatrix}$$

Thus, MATLAB solves systems of equations quickly and easily. In short, MATLAB takes all the computational work out of doing matrix algebra. This leaves the user free to think about what the algebra means and about alternative problem-solving strategies.

MATLAB FUNCTIONS

In addition to the elementary matrix operations of addition, subtraction, multiplication, and powers, the following matrix functions are available in MATLAB:

INV(A)	inverse
DET(A)	determinant
COND(A)	condition number
RCOND(A)	a measure of nearness to singularity
EIG(A)	eigenvalues and eigenvectors
SCHUR(A)	Schur triangular form
HESS(A)	Hessenburg or tridiagonal form
POLY(A)	characteristic polynomial
SVD(A)	singular value decomposition
PINV(A,eps)	pseudoinverse with optional tolerance
RANK(A,eps)	matrix rank with optional tolerance
LU(A)	factors from Gaussian elimination
CHOL(A)	factors from Cholesky factorization
QR(A)	factors from Householder orthogonaliza-tion
RREF(A)	reduced row echelon form
ORTH(A)	orthogonal vectors spanning range of A
EXP(A)	e raised to the power of A
LOG(A)	natural logarithm
SQRT(A)	square root
SIN(A)	trigonometric sine
COS(A)	cosine
ATAN(A)	arctangent
ROUND(A)	round elements to nearest integers
ABS(A)	absolute value of the elements

REAL(A)	real parts of the elements
IMAG(A)	imaginary parts of the elements
CONJG(A)	complex conjugate
SUM(A)	sum of the elements
PROD(A)	product of the elements
DIAG(A)	extract or create diagonal matrices
TRIL(A)	lower triangular part of A
TRIU(A)	upper triangular part of A
NORM(A,p)	norm with p =1, 2, or infinity
EYE(m,n)	portion of identity matrix
RAND(m,n)	matrix with random elements
ONES(m,n)	matrix of all 1's
MAGIC(n)	makes magic squares
HILBERT(n)	inverse Hilbert matrices
ROOTS(c)	roots of polynomial with coefficients c
DISPLAY(A,p)	print base p representation of A
KRON(A,B)	Kronecker tensor product of A and B
PLOT(X,Y)	plot Y as a function of X
RAT(A)	find simple rational approximation of A
USER(A)	function defined by external program

Commercial versions of MATLAB for IBM-compatible computers, Macintosh computers, and Unix-based graphics workstations are available from The MathWorks, Inc., Suite 250, 20 North Main St., Sherborn, MA 01770, (617) 653-1415. These versions offer many more matrix functions as well as outstanding graphics and editing features not available in MATLAB. For example, readers should be aware that the PLOT(X,Y) function in Public Brand Software's MATLAB offers only the crudest graphics and is of little practical value. The graphics available in the commercial versions of MATLAB are powerful and easy to use.

AN EXAMPLE USING MATLAB

Matrix algebra provides a convenient way to change reference systems. For instance, assume that a space shuttle must

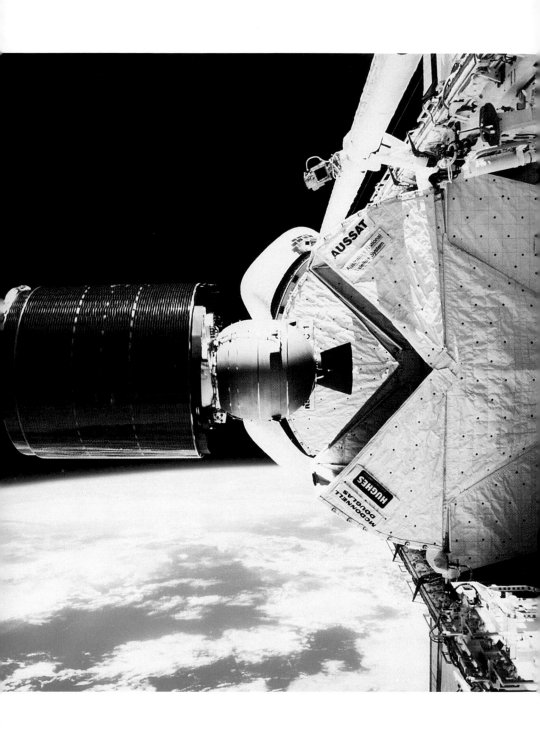

dock with an orbiting satellite. As the shuttle approaches the satellite, the shuttle performs a series of rotations to point the cargo bay directly at the satellite. With respect to the shuttle's reference system, the rotations move the satellite from one location to another in the "sky" so that it ends up directly over the cargo bay. Since the only way to avoid a collision is for the shuttle to "know" exactly where the satellite is at all times, the shuttle computers must constantly recalculate the satellite's position in the shuttle's reference system as the shuttle turns in space.

There are three types of rotations performed in air and space vehicles: roll, pitch, and yaw. A roll rotates the craft about its principal axis—a line from the nose to the tail of the craft. A pitch moves the nose up or down. And a yaw rotates the craft sideways with respect to its direction of motion.

The following MATLAB commands and matrices will put a series of rotations in matrix form. In the following example from Bernice Kastner's Space Mathematics, the shuttle undergoes a roll of R = 30 degrees, a pitch of P = 45 degrees, and a yaw of Y = 60 degrees.

```
R = 30
P = 45
Y = 60
```

These values are converted to radians as follows:

```
RR = R*3.14159/180
RP = P*3.14159/180
RY = Y*3.14159/180
```

A satellite exits the cargo bay of the space shuttle
***Discovery.* When it retrieves satellites for repair, the shuttle must perform a series of rotations to align the cargo bay with the satellite.**

Kastner derives transformation matrices to simplify the task of representing the algebraic relationships between old and new coordinates. Given the choice, many students prefer to work with the relatively simple form of such transformation matrices rather than to struggle with the system of algebraic statements that they represent.

$$
ROLL = \begin{bmatrix} 1 & 0 & 0 \\ 0 & \cos(RR) & \sin(RR) \\ 0 & -\sin(RR) & \cos(RR) \end{bmatrix}
$$

$$
PITCH = \begin{bmatrix} \cos(RP) & 0 & -\sin(RP) \\ 0 & 1 & 0 \\ \sin(RP) & 0 & \cos(RP) \end{bmatrix}
$$

$$
YAW = \begin{bmatrix} \cos(RY) & -\sin(RY) & 0 \\ \sin(RY) & \cos(RY) & 0 \\ 0 & 0 & 1 \end{bmatrix}
$$

Using these matrices and the given values for R, P, and Y, a sequence of rotations consisting of a roll of 30 degrees, a pitch of 45 degrees, and a yaw of 60 degrees may be represented as

RESULT = YAW*PITCH*ROLL

MATLAB yields the transformation matrix

$$
RESULT = \begin{bmatrix} .35 & .93 & .13 \\ -.61 & .13 & .78 \\ .71 & -.35 & .61 \end{bmatrix}
$$

This matrix may now be applied to any point in space in order to compute its location in the shuttle's reference system after the roll-pitch-yaw rotations. For example, the sequence of rotations described would move the point

(1, 2, 3) to the point (6.06, 1.99, 1.84) in the shuttle's reference system.

$$\text{RESULT} * \begin{bmatrix} 1 \\ 2 \\ 3 \end{bmatrix} = \begin{bmatrix} 6.06 \\ 1.99 \\ 1.84 \end{bmatrix}$$

By working in this way with a real-world problem, you can examine experimentally general questions about matrix operations, such as "Is matrix multiplication commutative?" Is a roll-pitch-yaw the same maneuver in general as a pitch-yaw-roll? A simple MATLAB test will give the answer—no. Does the inverse of the transformation RESULT have a physical meaning? The answer is yes; it is the transformation that reverses the effect of the transformation RESULT. These kinds of questions give substance to the abstract study of matrix algebra and tend to inspire further discussion.

Project 4.1
Programming in the MATLAB language, create a computer program that simulates how a fixed-star field would change its orientation in the space shuttle's frame of reference as the shuttle undergoes various roll-pitch-yaw maneuvers.

PEANUT SOFTWARE

A number of easy-to-use mathematics programs for IBM-compatible computers are available from Peanut Software, Richard Parris, Phillips Exeter Academy, Exeter, NH, 03833, Tel: (603) 772-1044. Since this software is perpetually in a state of revision, you may want to obtain an up-to-date copy by sending him a formatted diskette (360K, 720K, or 1.2M) and a self-addressed, stamped mailer.

One of the programs, GEOM, offers a variety of tools for

constructing and measuring 2-dimensional objects. Even 3-dimensional objects may be constructed and viewed in perspective. Similar in many ways to the Geometric Supposer software, GEOM supports a number of graphics drivers, allows files to be saved and reloaded, and can send images to your printer. A sample of a GEOM construction and measurement session is shown in Figure 4.1.

STATPAC is a basic probability and statistics package with nice graphics. Because of the limited number of distributions and statistical tests available, this is more of a beginner's program than a general research tool. A graphing package called PLOT is, like STATPAC, easy to use but somewhat limited in scope. However, if a basic graphing tool is all that is needed, this program generates nice graphics as shown in Figure 4.2. A number of other programs are available from

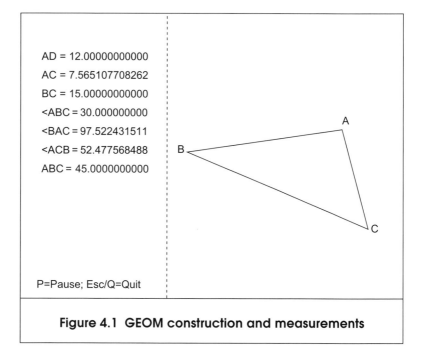

AD = 12.00000000000
AC = 7.565107708262
BC = 15.00000000000
<ABC = 30.000000000
<BAC = 97.522431511
<ACB = 52.477568488
ABC = 45.0000000000

P=Pause; Esc/Q=Quit

Figure 4.1 GEOM construction and measurements

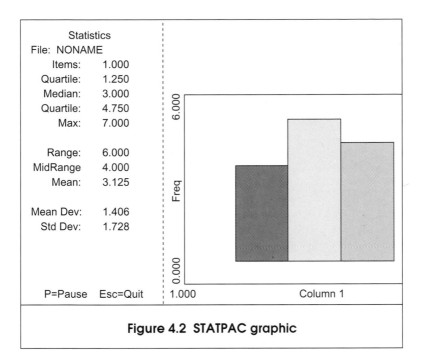

Figure 4.2 STATPAC graphic

Peanut Software, all of which have the same "look" with regard to graphical displays and require the same type of commands.

Chapter 8 looks at other computer packages that help visualize specific geometries discussed later in the book.

5

MATHEMATICAL FRIEZES

Some geometry studies offer students an opportunity to experience the creative interplay between mathematics and art. One of the best examples of that interplay is ornamental friezes.

Technically speaking, a frieze is a horizontal decorative band found in Grecian, Greco-Roman, and neo-classical architecture (see Figure 5.1). This kind of frieze is carved in relief in stone and often tells a story or commemorates a victory. You may have seen friezes on the facades of historic buildings or in archaeology books, as well as on stationery, decorative paper, magazines, and other publications. When used for strictly ornamental purposes, friezes repeat a particular design (motif) over and over.

Believe it or not, these repetitive friezes have distinct mathematical properties. Every ornamental frieze may be characterized by the symmetries of its fundamental motif. The following terminology helps describe those symmetries:

• A *centerline* is a horizontal line running through the middle of the frieze.

This architectural frieze on the National Building
Museum in Washington, D.C., has the repetitive
character of mathematical friezes.

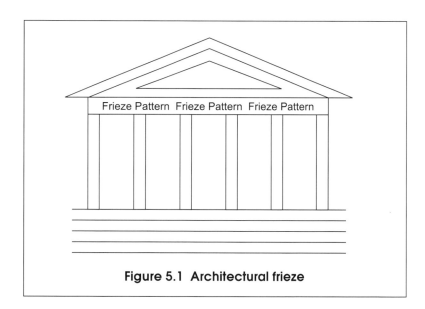

Figure 5.1 Architectural frieze

- A *point of symmetry* is a point about which a motif may be rotated 180 degrees without changing its appearance.
- A *line of symmetry* divides the figure into two parts, each a mirror image of the other.

In learning the concept of a frieze, it helps to begin with friezes constructed from letters of the alphabet. For example, the sequence of letters TTTTT may be thought of as a frieze. The frieze motif, the letter T, has a line of symmetry perpendicular to the centerline. The frieze HOHOHO repeats a pair of objects, the letters H and O. The frieze motif, HO, has the centerline as a line of symmetry. The frieze NNN repeats the letter N, which has a point of symmetry. In fact, any repeating sequence of letters may be thought of as a frieze. Of course, some motifs have more interesting symmetries than others. What symmetries do you see in the following friezes?

SOSSOSSO
ΛVΛVΛVΛV
DODODODO
/\/\/\/\/\
UUUUUUUU
AMAMAMAM
MATHMATH

Clearly, there are infinitely many motifs that could be the basis of a frieze. But what of the symmetries exhibited by these many motifs? As it turns out, there are only seven possible combinations of symmetries that a frieze can exhibit. Figure 5.2 shows seven frieze symmetry patterns. It can be shown that every frieze has the symmetry characteristics of one of these seven frieze patterns (see the 1989 book *A Course in Modern Geometries* by Judith Cederberg).

Pattern F1 represents motifs like the letter L that have no points or lines of symmetry.

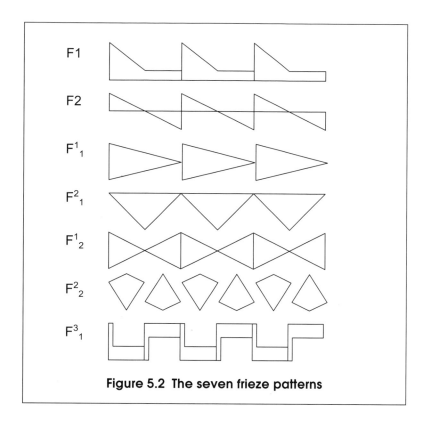

Figure 5.2 The seven frieze patterns

Pattern F2 represents motifs like the letter N that have a point of symmetry.

Pattern F^1_1 motifs, such as the letter D, have a centerline as a line of symmetry but no point of symmetry.

Pattern F^2_1 motifs, such as the letter V or T, have a line of symmetry perpendicular to the centerline at the midpoint of the motif. They have no point of symmetry.

Pattern F^1_2 motifs include the letter H, with a point of symmetry and symmetry about the centerline. As a consequence of these two symmetries, there is a second line of symmetry perpendicular to the centerline at the midpoint of the motif.

Pattern F^2_2 has a point of symmetry in the middle of the motif. In the completed frieze pattern, there is also a line of symmetry perpendicular to the centerline at a point $\frac{1}{4}$ of the distance across each motif. The pair of objects ∧∨ is an example of this kind of motif.

The final pattern, F^3_1, is a glide reflection; that means the motif can be created by reflecting an object about its centerline and shifting the result to the right of the original object. The resulting motif, however, has no points or lines of symmetry.

To check for lines of symmetry, reflect the object across the line and see whether you get what you started with. To check for a point of symmetry, make a half-turn—spin the motif 180 degrees—and see whether you get the original motif. Typically, to avoid mistakes, these reflections and half-turns are incorporated into the process of generating the frieze patterns. For example, pattern F1 friezes are generated by making a half-turn in the motif and translating it to the right a distance τ, the width of the motif. Note that the original objects are always translated to the right by τ, except in pattern F^3_1, when the object is reflected about the centerline and then shifted to the right by $\frac{\tau}{2}$.

Figure 5.3 shows a method adapted from George Martin's 1982 book *Transformation Geometry* for determining to which frieze pattern a particular frieze belongs. The method classifies friezes according to their generating process and starts with the question "Is there a half-turn?" If the answer is no, move to the left in the flow chart; otherwise move to the right. The questions continue, checking for other symmetries and guiding you to the correct pattern.

FRIEZES, ISOMETRIES, AND LINEAR TRANSFORMATIONS

You may have already guessed how friezes are related to linear transformations. Whenever an object is moved, copied, or reoriented in the Euclidean plane, we say that the object has undergone a transformation. As you learned earlier, if the transformation preserves collinearity (the image of a

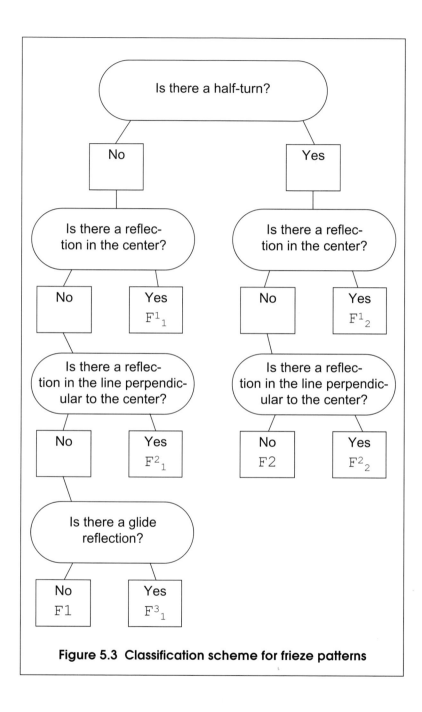

Figure 5.3 Classification scheme for frieze patterns

straight line is a straight line) and concurrence (the image of a pair of intersecting lines is a pair of intersecting lines), then we call the transformation linear. We have also seen that not all linear transformations preserve the size and shape of an object. Some involve stretching or shearing, often producing images that bear little resemblance to the objects from which they came.

Isometries, on the other hand, are linear transformations that preserve the linear and angular measures of the objects to which they are applied. Another way to think about isometries is that they generate images that are congruent with the original object. Since friezes repeat the same basic pattern over and over, the linear transformations associated with friezes are classified as isometries. Every isometry has a matrix with one of the following forms,

$$
\begin{bmatrix} a & b & c \\ -b & a & d \\ 0 & 0 & 1 \end{bmatrix} \quad or \quad \begin{bmatrix} a & b & c \\ b & -a & d \\ 0 & 0 & 1 \end{bmatrix}
$$

where $a^2 + b^2 = 1$. All translations, rotations, reflections, and glide reflections can be represented by such matrices.

FRIEZE PATTERNS AND TRANSFORMATION MATRICES

In developing matrix representations for the seven frieze patterns, we must adopt a convention to characterize translations and points and lines of symmetry. Our convention uses the nomenclature defined in Figure 5.4.

According to this nomenclature, a translation τ may be represented by the matrix

$$
\tau = \begin{bmatrix} 1 & 0 & 2c_1 \\ 0 & 1 & 0 \\ 0 & 0 & 1 \end{bmatrix}
$$

where $\tau = 2c_1$.

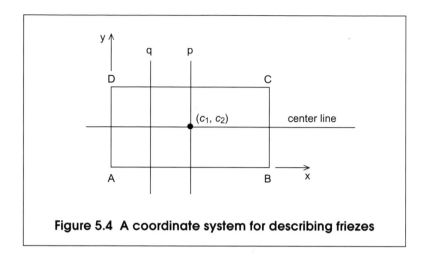

Figure 5.4 A coordinate system for describing friezes

The symmetry transformation consisting of a half-turn about the point $c = (c_1, c_2)$ is represented by the matrix

$$H_c = \begin{bmatrix} -1 & 0 & 2c_1 \\ 0 & -1 & 2c_2 \\ 0 & 0 & 1 \end{bmatrix}$$

The symmetry transformation consisting of a reflection about the center line $y = c_2$ may be represented by

$$R_c = \begin{bmatrix} 1 & 0 & 0 \\ 0 & -1 & 2c_2 \\ 0 & 0 & 1 \end{bmatrix}$$

Two other symmetries involve reflections about lines perpendicular to the centerline. One reflection, R_p, centers on the line $x = c_1$. It is represented by the matrix

$$R_p = \begin{bmatrix} -1 & 0 & 2c_1 \\ 0 & 1 & 0 \\ 0 & 0 & 1 \end{bmatrix}$$

The reflection R_q about the line $x = \dfrac{c_1}{2}$ is:

$$R_q = \begin{bmatrix} \text{-1} & 0 & c_1 \\ 0 & 1 & 0 \\ 0 & 0 & 1 \end{bmatrix}$$

Now let's apply the symmetry transformations to the shaded object in Figure 5.5 to determine mathematically the frieze pattern to which it belongs. If $c_1 = 1$ and $c_2 = 0.5$, each of the symmetry transformations listed previously may be written as follows:

$$H_c = \begin{bmatrix} \text{-1} & 0 & 2 \\ 0 & \text{-1} & 0 \\ 0 & 0 & 1 \end{bmatrix}$$

$$R_c = \begin{bmatrix} 1 & 0 & 0 \\ 0 & \text{-1} & 1 \\ 0 & 0 & 1 \end{bmatrix}$$

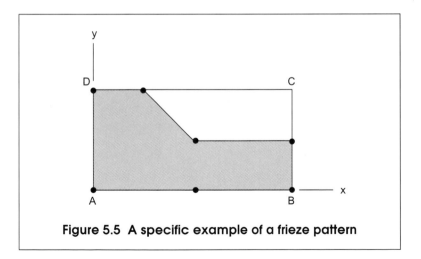

Figure 5.5 A specific example of a frieze pattern

$$R_p = \begin{bmatrix} -1 & 0 & 2 \\ 0 & 1 & 0 \\ 0 & 0 & 1 \end{bmatrix}$$

$$R_q = \begin{bmatrix} -1 & 0 & 1 \\ 0 & 1 & 0 \\ 0 & 0 & 1 \end{bmatrix}$$

To see the effect of each of these transformations on the shaded object in Figure 5.5, we must create a matrix representing the object. This matrix X consists of seven column vectors, each representing one of seven points along the object's boundary.

$$X = \begin{bmatrix} 0 & 1 & 2 & 2 & 1 & .5 & 0 \\ 0 & 0 & 0 & .5 & .5 & 1 & 1 \\ 1 & 1 & 1 & 1 & 1 & 1 & 1 \end{bmatrix}$$

We can now determine whether the shaded figure has any of the symmetries by computing the image of X after it undergoes each of the symmetry transformations. If the transformed object has the same points as the original object, then the object has the corresponding symmetry. Otherwise, the object does not have the symmetry in question. When X is transformed with matrices H_c, R_c, R_p, and R_q, the following results are obtained:

$$H_c * X = \begin{bmatrix} 2 & 1 & 0 & 0 & 1 & 1.5 & 2 \\ 0 & 0 & 0 & -.5 & -.5 & -1 & -1 \\ 1 & 1 & 1 & 1 & 1 & 1 & 1 \end{bmatrix}$$

$$R_c * X = \begin{bmatrix} 0 & 1 & 2 & 2 & 1 & .5 & 0 \\ 1 & 1 & 1 & .5 & .5 & 0 & 0 \\ 1 & 1 & 1 & 1 & 1 & 1 & 1 \end{bmatrix}$$

$$R_p*X = \begin{bmatrix} 2 & 1 & 0 & 0 & 1 & 1.5 & 2 \\ 0 & 0 & 0 & .5 & .5 & 1 & 1 \\ 1 & 1 & 1 & 1 & 1 & 1 & 1 \end{bmatrix}$$

$$R_q*X = \begin{bmatrix} 1 & 0 & -1 & -1 & 0 & .5 & 1 \\ 0 & 0 & 0 & .5 & .5 & 1 & 1 \\ 1 & 1 & 1 & 1 & 1 & 1 & 1 \end{bmatrix}$$

None of the transformed matrices contains the identical points found in X, so the shaded object has none of the symmetries under consideration. This observation "checks" with a visual inspection of the object. Thus, the object must belong to symmetry pattern F1.

If a triangle represented by

$$Y \quad = \begin{bmatrix} 0 & 2 & 1 \\ 0 & 0 & 1 \\ 1 & 1 & 1 \end{bmatrix}$$

is "tested" in the same manner, however, a symmetry is revealed.

$$H_c*Y = \begin{bmatrix} 2 & 0 & 1 \\ 0 & 0 & -1 \\ 1 & 1 & 1 \end{bmatrix}$$

$$R_c*Y = \begin{bmatrix} 0 & 2 & 1 \\ 1 & 1 & 0 \\ 1 & 1 & 1 \end{bmatrix}$$

$$R_p*Y = \begin{bmatrix} 2 & 0 & 1 \\ 0 & 0 & 1 \\ 1 & 1 & 1 \end{bmatrix}$$

$$R_q*Y = \begin{bmatrix} 1 & -1 & 0 \\ 0 & 0 & 1 \\ 1 & 1 & 1 \end{bmatrix}$$

In this case, one of the transformed matrices is equivalent to the original set Y. Although the order of the points in each matrix is different, the points in matrix Y are identical to those in R_p*Y : (2, 0, 1), (0, 0, 1), and (1, 1 ,1). This means the triangle has a line of symmetry, p, perpendicular to the center line. A visual inspection corroborates our result. Thus, the object belongs to pattern $F2_1$.

Using transformation matrices as building blocks, we can construct a matrix representation for each frieze pattern.

$$F_1: \tau \quad = \begin{bmatrix} 1 & 0 & 2c_1 \\ 0 & 1 & 0 \\ 0 & 0 & 1 \end{bmatrix}$$

$$F_2: \tau*H_c \quad = \begin{bmatrix} 1 & 0 & 2c_1 \\ 0 & 1 & 0 \\ 0 & 0 & 1 \end{bmatrix} \begin{bmatrix} -1 & 0 & 2c_1 \\ 0 & -1 & 2c_2 \\ 0 & 0 & 1 \end{bmatrix} = \begin{bmatrix} -1 & 0 & 4c_1 \\ 0 & -1 & 2c_2 \\ 0 & 0 & 1 \end{bmatrix}$$

$$F^1_1: \tau*R_c \quad = \begin{bmatrix} 1 & 0 & 2c_1 \\ 0 & 1 & 0 \\ 0 & 0 & 1 \end{bmatrix} \begin{bmatrix} 1 & 0 & 0 \\ 0 & -1 & 2c_2 \\ 0 & 0 & 1 \end{bmatrix} = \begin{bmatrix} 1 & 0 & 2c_1 \\ 0 & -1 & 2c_2 \\ 0 & 0 & 1 \end{bmatrix}$$

$$F^2_1: \tau*R_p \quad = \begin{bmatrix} 1 & 0 & 2c_1 \\ 0 & 1 & 0 \\ 0 & 0 & 1 \end{bmatrix} \begin{bmatrix} -1 & 0 & 2c_1 \\ 0 & 1 & 0 \\ 0 & 0 & 1 \end{bmatrix} = \begin{bmatrix} -1 & 0 & 4c_1 \\ 0 & 1 & 0 \\ 0 & 0 & 1 \end{bmatrix}$$

$$F^1_2: \tau*H_c*R_c = \begin{bmatrix} 1 & 0 & 2c_1 \\ 0 & 1 & 0 \\ 0 & 0 & 1 \end{bmatrix} \begin{bmatrix} -1 & 0 & 2c_1 \\ 0 & -1 & 2c_2 \\ 0 & 0 & 1 \end{bmatrix} \begin{bmatrix} 1 & 0 & 0 \\ 0 & -1 & 2c_2 \\ 0 & 0 & 1 \end{bmatrix} = \begin{bmatrix} -1 & 0 & 4c_1 \\ 0 & 1 & 0 \\ 0 & 0 & 1 \end{bmatrix}$$

$$F^2_2: \tau*H_c*R_q = \begin{bmatrix} 1 & 0 & 2c_1 \\ 0 & 1 & 0 \\ 0 & 0 & 1 \end{bmatrix} \begin{bmatrix} -1 & 0 & 2c_1 \\ 0 & -1 & 2c_2 \\ 0 & 0 & 1 \end{bmatrix} \begin{bmatrix} -1 & 0 & c_2 \\ 0 & 1 & 0 \\ 0 & 0 & 1 \end{bmatrix} = \begin{bmatrix} 1 & 0 & 3c_1 \\ 0 & -1 & 2c_2 \\ 0 & 0 & 1 \end{bmatrix}$$

$$F^3_1: \sigma \quad = \begin{bmatrix} 1 & 0 & c_1 \\ 0 & 1 & 0 \\ 0 & 0 & 1 \end{bmatrix} \text{ where } \sigma^2 = \tau$$

These matrices may now be applied to specific motifs inscribed inside rectangle ABCD. If the motif belongs to the class the matrix represents, the matrix operation will move the motif τ units to the right of point A. To extend the frieze further, the transformation must be repeatedly applied to the original motif, with powers of τ increasing incrementally. For example, extending a frieze in pattern F2 would require that the following sequence of matrices be applied: τH_c, $\tau^2 H_c$, $\tau^3 H_c$, and so on.

If you suddenly insert a different symmetry transformation, you normally break the repetitive pattern of the frieze. That may sound like common sense, but there is an interesting exception to this rule. You may have noticed that two of the frieze patterns, F^2_1 and F^1_2, have the same resultant matrix; thus, both matrix representations would extend the frieze of either pattern properly.

Why are two patterns with different symmetries represented by the same matrix? The answer may help you understand better how frieze patterns differ from each other. Let's look at the example of the letter V, which belongs to pattern F^2_1, and the letter H, which belongs to pattern F^1_2.

If we apply the symmetry transformations of H's pattern to V, the letter is first inverted by the R_c reflection and then spun upright again by the half-turn H_c. Thus, the final result is correct, but the object fails to retain its original appearance throughout the transformation process. To qualify for a frieze pattern, the object must not change in appearance during any of the symmetry transformations for the pattern. That's because the motifs of the seven patterns are visually distinct by virtue of their symmetries—not the outcome of their transformations.

Once familiar with the properties of the seven frieze patterns, you may design your own friezes and classify friezes created by your classmates. Working on grid paper makes it easy to block out the location of subsequent elements in the frieze and provides horizontal and vertical guides for reflecting lines. To simplify drawing the reflection of an object

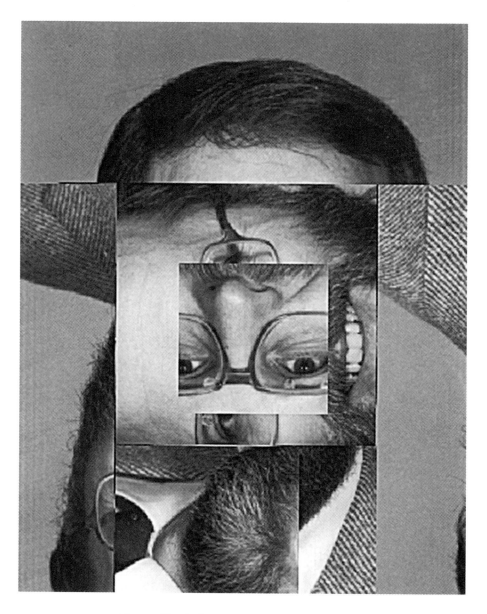

The author's face was rearranged using
isometries, linear transformations in which objects
are translated, rotated, and reflected.

in a line of symmetry, get a Mira, a device available in most school mathematics departments for drawing reflections. Or if you have a computer "paint" program, which automatically translates, reflects, and rotates selected objects, it can do the work for you.

The study of frieze patterns offers students the opportunity to investigate the mathematical properties of objects that also have artistic, historic, and social significance. An exploration of the friezes favored by various cultural, religious, and ethnic groups, for example, could be used as the basis for cross-cultural studies linking mathematics, social studies, and art. A contest to design friezes could lead to interesting new borders for bulletin boards and school newsletters. Just think of the meaningful connections and applications of friezes you could discover!

Project 5.1
Write a computer program that can generate a frieze using any 2-dimensional figure as a motif.

Project 5.2
With a PC "paint" program, create frieze patterns suitable for decorative purposes in a variety of settings.

6

OTHER APPLICATIONS
OF MATRICES

AN INTRODUCTION TO GRAPH THEORY

Mathematicians use graph theory to model the relationships among a finite set of objects.

When applied to social or business problems, these objects may consist of people, institutions, airline routes, sports teams, or many other entities. For example, Figure 6.1 is a finite graph that shows the results of a round-robin ping-pong tournament involving four teams, $T_1 - T_4$.

The graph should be read as follows. An arrow from T_i to T_j indicates that team i beat team j. For team T_1, the arrows indicate that team 1 beat teams 2 and 4, but lost to team 3.

Similar statements can be made regarding the performance of teams 2, 3, and 4. The results can be represented more concisely in what is known as the adjacency matrix, A:

$$A = \begin{bmatrix} 0 & 1 & 0 & 1 \\ 0 & 0 & 1 & 0 \\ 1 & 0 & 0 & 1 \\ 0 & 1 & 0 & 0 \end{bmatrix}$$

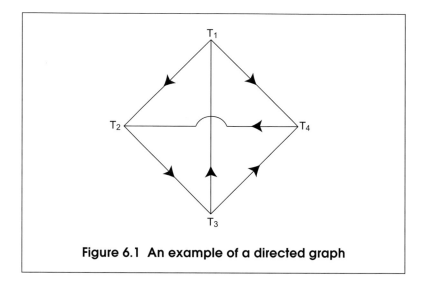

Figure 6.1 An example of a directed graph

If team i beat team j, then a 1 is entered in row i and column j of the matrix. In this convention, the teams beaten by team i are indicated by a 1 in row i in the losing team's column. A glance at the matrix reveals that two teams won two games each and two teams won one game apiece. How should the teams be ranked if no ties are allowed?

The answer may be found in the concept of powerful points. They are points having arrows pointing toward every other point on the graph, on either a direct path or an indirect path through another point. In terms of the sports analogy, this is equivalent to saying a team is powerful if it beat every other team or if it beat a team that beat the other teams. Powerful points can be determined by squaring matrix A and adding the result to A.

$$A + A^2 = \begin{bmatrix} 0 & 2 & 1 & 1 \\ 1 & 0 & 1 & 1 \\ 1 & 2 & 0 & 2 \\ 0 & 1 & 1 & 0 \end{bmatrix}$$

To determine the power of each team, add the entries in its row in the matrix: team 1 has a power of 4, team 2 has a power of 3, team 3 has a power of 5, and team 4 has a power of 2.

According to these scores, the final rankings in the tournament should be:

First place	team 3
Second place	team 1
Third place	team 2
Fourth place	team 4

There are many other situations in which graph theory techniques may be applied. The following projects explore a few of them:

Project 6.1
Look for opportunities to model team competitions at school using finite graphs. Debate teams, tennis teams, and many others participate in round-robin tournaments. Develop a computer program that will correctly interpret the results of these tournaments.

Project 6.2
Graph theory can also model the spread of a disease or contaminants among a group of workers or other people who come into contact with one another in well-defined ways. Making specific assumptions, develop a model to study the spread of a contagious disease such as mononucleosis among students at your school.

Project 6.3
The political or social influence exerted by a small group of activists can also be modeled. Develop a model of influence in your town or school based on specific assumptions. Where circumstances allow, test your model's predictions against reality.

PROJECTIVE GEOMETRY

Analytic geometry has always been more than an intellectual exercise. Geometric principles have been applied to engineering, science, art, and other disciplines. And new geometric questions have arisen as a result. One of the most important applications of geometry to art occurred at the beginning of the Renaissance when geometric perspective began to appear in drawings and paintings. Two-dimensional art could, at last, look "real." This development also made possible realistic architectural renderings. More recently, projective geometry has brought geometric perspective to the world of computer graphics.

Engineers and architects use projective geometry to create realistic displays of 3-dimensional objects on 2-dimensional computer screens. Figure 6.2 is a perspective projection of a building. In perspective projections, parallel lines on a

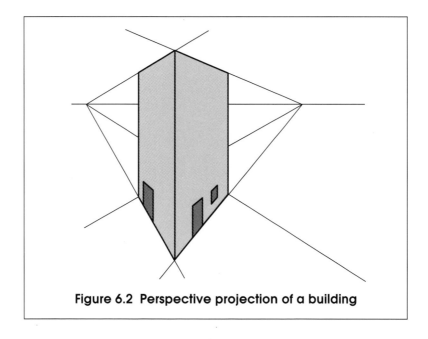

Figure 6.2 Perspective projection of a building

3-dimensional object appear to converge at vanishing points. A good reference for readers interested in pursuing this topic is *Mathematical Elements for Computer Graphics*, 2nd edition, by David F. Rogers and J. Alan Adams.

In 3-point perspective projections, a 3-dimensional object, such as a cube, is positioned in a reference system as shown in Figure 6.3. The vertices of the cube are assigned coordinates of the form $(x, y, z, 1)$ in order to facilitate matrix representation. Using this convention, the eight vertices of the cube may be represented in a matrix X, where each column represents the coordinates of one vertex.

$$X = \begin{bmatrix} 0 & 1 & 1 & 0 & 0 & 1 & 1 & 0 \\ 0 & 0 & 1 & 1 & 0 & 0 & 1 & 1 \\ 1 & 1 & 1 & 1 & 0 & 0 & 0 & 0 \\ 1 & 1 & 1 & 1 & 1 & 1 & 1 & 1 \end{bmatrix}$$

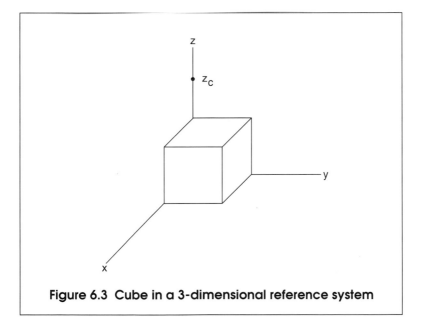

Figure 6.3 Cube in a 3-dimensional reference system

In this approach, the viewer is always positioned at a point Z_c, called the center of the projection. Z_c is some distance away from the object on the Z-axis. From such a position, only one face of the cube would be visible, bounded by the four vertices (1, 0, 1, 1), (0, 0, 1, 1), (0, 1, 1, 1), and (1, 1, 1, 1). To expose two additional faces of the cube to get a better view, we could rotate it θ degrees about the X-axis and ϕ degrees about the Y-axis. The rotated cube may then be projected onto the plane Z = 0, the XY plane.

The transformation matrix P that accomplishes both rotations and the projection onto the Z = 0 plane is

$$
P = \begin{bmatrix}
\cos\phi & 0 & \sin\phi & 0 \\
\sin\phi\sin\theta & \cos\theta & -\cos\phi\sin\theta & 0 \\
0 & 0 & 0 & 0 \\
\dfrac{\sin\phi\cos\theta}{Z_c} & \dfrac{-\sin\phi}{Z_c} & \dfrac{-\cos\phi\cos\theta}{Z_c} & 1
\end{bmatrix}
$$

If $\theta = 45$ and $\phi = -30$, and if $Z_c = 2.5$, then

$$
P = \begin{bmatrix}
.8660 & 0 & -.5000 & 0 \\
-.3536 & .7071 & -.6124 & 0 \\
0 & 0 & 0 & 0 \\
-.1414 & -.2828 & -.2449 & 1
\end{bmatrix} \quad \text{and}
$$

$$
P*X = \begin{bmatrix}
-.5000 & .3660 & .3660 & -.5000 & 0 & .8660 & .8660 & 0 \\
-.6124 & -.9659 & -.2588 & .0947 & 0 & -.3536 & .3536 & .7071 \\
0 & 0 & 0 & 0 & 0 & 0 & 0 & 0 \\
.7551 & .6136 & .3308 & .4722 & 1 & .8586 & .5757 & .7172
\end{bmatrix}
$$

Each column corresponds to a vertex of the transformed cube. But since a point in Euclidean 3-dimensional space must have coordinates of the form (x, y, z, 1), each set of coordinates must be divided by the last number in the column to make the final coordinate 1. When that task is done, the transformed coordinates of the cube are

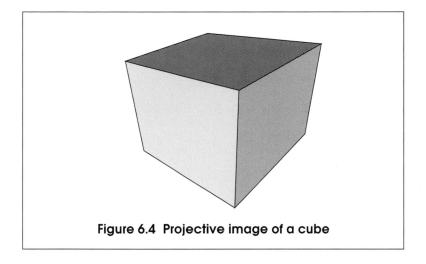

Figure 6.4 Projective image of a cube

$$\begin{bmatrix} -.6622 & .5965 & 1.1065 & -1.0589 & 0 & 1.0087 & 1.5042 & 0 \\ -.8110 & -1.5741 & -.7824 & .2006 & 0 & -.4118 & .6141 & .9860 \\ 0 & 0 & 0 & 0 & 0 & 0 & 0 & 0 \\ 1 & 1 & 1 & 1 & 1 & 1 & 1 & 1 \end{bmatrix}$$

Notice that the z-coordinate of each point is 0, which means all the points lie in the XY plane—the goal of the exercise. When the points are plotted and connected, the projective image of the cube appears as shown in Figure 6.4.

This method, which will create perspective drawings of any 3-dimensional object, can be explored further in the following projects.

Project 6.4

Create a computer program that can show perspective views of any 3-dimensional wire frame object from any point outside the object. Investigate the problems that arise when you try to show a perspective view of an object from inside the object. This problem had to be solved to create the

Projective geometry techniques can create the appropriate perspective in scenes like this one from the Disney movie _Beauty and the Beast_.

interior scenes in the animated feature film _Beauty and the Beast_.

Project 6.5
Create a computer program that enables the viewer to "zoom in" on some wire frame object by changing the cen-

ter of the projection, Z_c. Animate the zoom by making a series of images in which Z_c moves closer and closer to the object.

Project 6.6
It is possible to project a 3-dimensional object onto the surface of a sphere rather than onto a flat surface like the XY plane. Create a computer program to demonstrate this type of projection.

Project 6.7
Investigate projections onto other curved surfaces, such as saddles or ellipsoids.

ADVANCED PROJECTS INVOLVING MATRIX ALGEBRA

Here are other topics worth considering for the advanced student who is interested in applications of matrix algebra. These projects assume the student has a prior grounding in the topic.

Project 6.8
In finite Markov processes, the matrix entries are probabilities. One application of these processes is the simulation of "war games." Develop a computer program that will enable you to experiment with Markov processes and to simulate a battle.

Project 6.9
One of the most famous topics in matrix algebra is the eigenproblem, which is to find solutions to the equation $Ax = \lambda x$, where A is an $n \times n$ matrix and λ is a scalar. Investigate the relationship between the eigenvalues and eigenvectors of a linear transformation and the invariant features of the Euclidean plane under the transformation.

7

GEOMETRY AND
TOPOLOGY PROJECTS

The study of geometry has its roots in Eastern cultures that existed long ago. Yet for thousands of years, it has served as a foundation of Western thought and as a powerful tool for the shaping of young minds. Thanks to a renewed interest in geometry in the last few years, students today are once again exploring 2- and 3-dimensional space through the study of Euclidean forms and transformations, as discussed in Chapters 3 through 6. The projects in this chapter expand on the ideas in the previous chapters and provide many opportunities to connect geometry with other branches of mathematics.

INVESTIGATING AREA

Project 7.1
Figure 7.1 illustrates the concept of a skew square. Skew squares are constructed on a rectangular grid of points that are evenly spaced and that have integers for coordinates. The squares are skewed with respect to the grid, and each

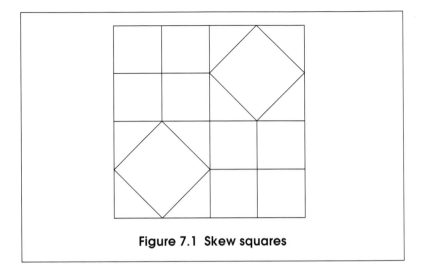

Figure 7.1 Skew squares

corner of a skew square must fall on one of the grid points. This construction creates small right triangles around the square. Each side of the square is the hypotenuse of a triangle, and two perpendicular grid segments of length a and b are the sides of the triangle. Knowing the lengths of these sides, it is easy to compute the hypotenuse c using the Pythagorean theorem, $a^2 + b^2 = c^2$. With that value, you can calculate the area of the skew square.

Every square constructed in this manner will have an integer as its area. Draw every skew square you can that has an area less than or equal to 100. Order these squares by their areas.

• Which whole numbers less than or equal to 100 represent areas of skew squares?

• Which do not represent areas of skew squares?

• Do prime numbers have anything to do with skew squares?

• Find a rule that will tell you whether a particular whole number of any size represents the area of a skew square.

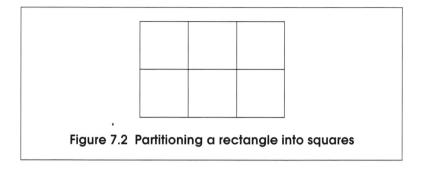

Figure 7.2 Partitioning a rectangle into squares

Project 7.2

A rectangle constructed on the integer coordinate grid may be divided into smaller integer squares, all of which are the same size, as shown in Figure 7.2. Investigate whether it is possible to

• subdivide a rectangle into squares so that no two squares are the same size;

• subdivide a square into squares so that no two smaller squares are the same size.

Project 7.3

A square or a cube may be divided into *n* smaller squares or cubes of various sizes (some of them may be the same size, as in Figure 7.3). For what values of *n* is this possible?

Project 7.4

It is obvious that squares of the same size will cover a plane without gaps or overlaps. As mathematicians put it, congruent squares are capable of tiling the plane. Is it possible to tile the plane with squares, no two of which are the same size, as in Figure 7.4?

Project 7.5

Some *m* x *n* rectangles may be tiled with smaller *p* x *q* rectangles as in Figure 7.5. Under what circumstances is this possible?

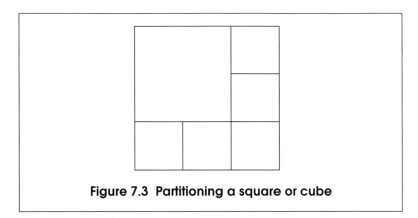

Figure 7.3 Partitioning a square or cube

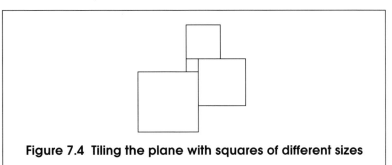

Figure 7.4 Tiling the plane with squares of different sizes

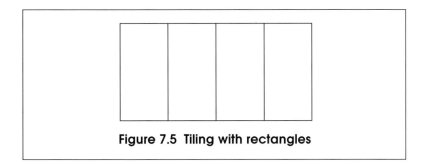

Figure 7.5 Tiling with rectangles

Project 7.6

The plane may be tiled with congruent equilateral triangles, as in Figure 7.6. Is it possible to tile the plane using equilateral triangles, no two of which are the same size?

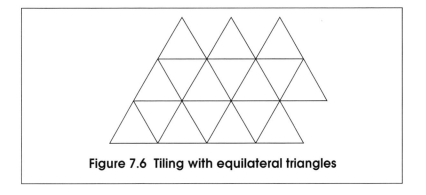

Figure 7.6 Tiling with equilateral triangles

Project 7.7

An *n*-reptile is a two-dimensional closed region that can be tiled with *n* congruent tiles that have the same shape as the *n*-reptile (see Figure 7.7). Fractiles are reptiles with fractal curves for boundaries. Develop a general approach for creating and classifying

  • convex reptiles; that is, reptiles with interior angles less than 180 degrees;
  • non-convex reptiles;
  • fractiles.

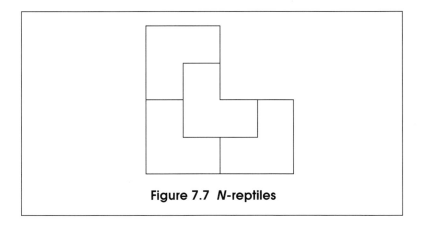

Figure 7.7 *N*-reptiles

Tiling of the plane can be accomplished with software such as RepTiles. One result from this program is shown here.

Project 7.8

Let R be any smooth or polygonal closed convex region. It should be possible to divide R into two regions of equal area by drawing a curve across R as shown in Figure 7.8. Find a method to accomplish this division with the shortest dividing curve possible.

Project 7.9

Let ABCD be a rectangle. Randomly select points P, Q, R, and S so that each is located on a different side of rectangle ABCD as shown in Figure 7.9. Connect P, Q, R, and S to form a quadrilateral. Express the area of quadrilateral PQRS as a percentage of the area of rectangle ABCD. Investigate the

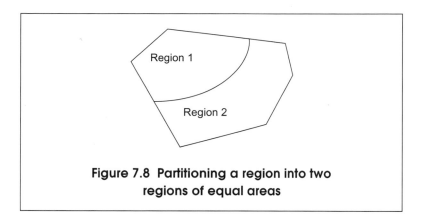

Figure 7.8 Partitioning a region into two regions of equal areas

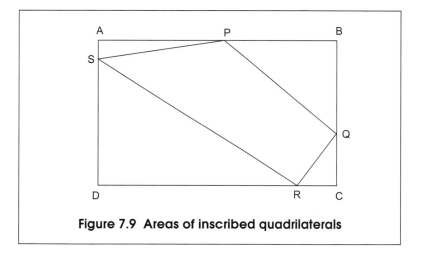

Figure 7.9 Areas of inscribed quadrilaterals

distribution of such areas for a given rectangle ABCD. Is the distribution dependent on the dimensions of ABCD?

Project 7.10

Follow the same general procedure as in Project 7.9 to investigate a triangle ABC with an inscribed triangle PQR, as shown in Figure 7.10.

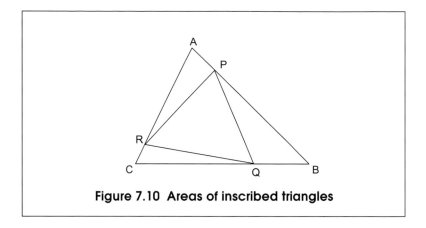

Figure 7.10 Areas of inscribed triangles

INVESTIGATING CURVES

Project 7.11

Define two types of regions in the plane by drawing
- a smooth convex closed curve, S; and
- a convex polygon with *n* sides, P.

Think of each region as a kind of frictionless air hockey table, with the boundary of the curve the reflecting or rebounding wall (see Figure 7.11). On this table, a puck striking the curve rebounds at an angle equal to the angle of

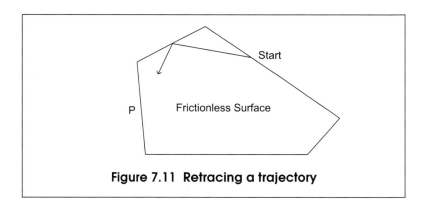

Figure 7.11 Retracing a trajectory

incidence—the angle the incoming puck makes with a perpendicular line (a normal) at the point of contact. Assuming
no friction, a puck launched in any direction will continue
bouncing around inside the region forever. In the case of the
curve P, assume that a puck striking a vertex of the polygon
rebounds along the bisector of the vertex angle, no matter
what the angle of incidence.

Which combinations of boundary curve, starting point,
and starting direction will cause a puck to retrace all or part
of its trajectory (revisit the same sequence of boundary points)
at some point in its journey?

Project 7.12
A curve is to be drawn on a sphere so that no point on the
sphere is farther than ε units from the curve. The "apple-peeling" spiral in Figure 7.12 is an example of such a curve. Find
other curves that meet this criterion. Is the "apple-peeling"
spiral the shortest possible curve?

Project 7.13
Given any simple closed curve C in the plane, it is obvious
that several points can be connected by segments to form

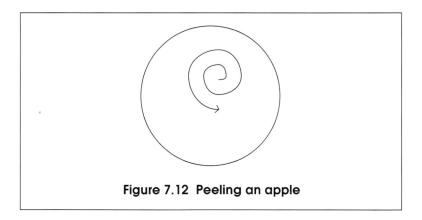

Figure 7.12 Peeling an apple

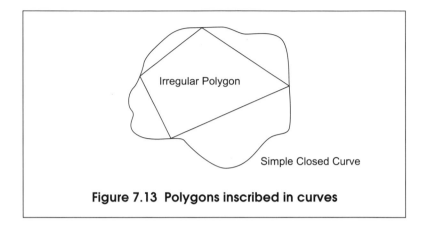

Figure 7.13 Polygons inscribed in curves

an irregular polygon, as in Figure 7.13. But is it always possible to find three points on C that are the vertices of an equilateral triangle? A parallelogram? A square? Investigate the question for convex curves first, then expand your investigation to include non-convex curves.

INVESTIGATING 3-DIMENSIONAL OBJECTS

Project 7.14
Let O represent a 3-dimensional convex object, such as a football or pyramid. A projection of O onto a sheet of paper would be equivalent to the shadow produced by a light source, as shown in Figure 7.14. The shadow may be represented by the closed 2-dimensional convex region S. Different shadows S may be obtained by rotating the object O in place. What can you learn about O from each shadow S, and how would you approach gathering information about the object O?

Project 7.15
A toroidal (doughnut-shaped) polyhedron may be constructed with many faces as in Figure 7.15. Each face is a

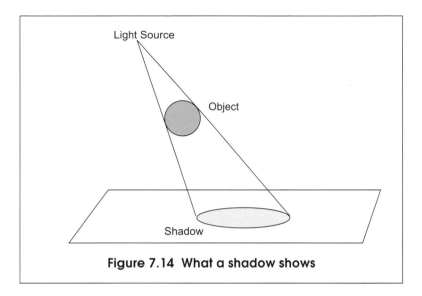

Figure 7.14 What a shadow shows

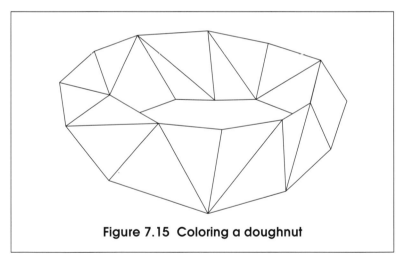

Figure 7.15 Coloring a doughnut

polygon that shares edges with adjacent faces. What is the minimum number of colors needed to color any toroidal polyhedron so that no two adjacent faces are the same color?

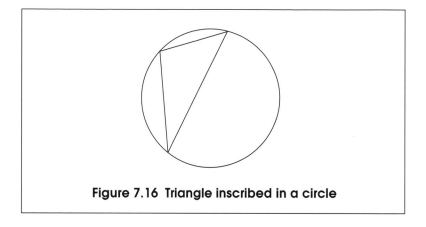

Figure 7.16 Triangle inscribed in a circle

Project 7.16

The following problems progress from specific cases to the general case. Answer each question before proceeding to the next.

• Three points on a 2-dimensional circle are selected at random and joined by segments to form a triangle, as in Figure 7.16. Find the probability that the center of the circle is inside the triangle.

• Four points on the surface of a 3-dimensional sphere are selected at random and joined with segments to form a tetrahedron as in Figure 7.17. What is the probability that the center of the sphere is inside the tetrahedron?

• $n + 1$ points are selected at random from the surface of an n-dimensional sphere. The points are connected, forming an n-dimensional convex hull called a simplex. What is the probability that the center of the n-dimensional sphere is inside the n-dimensional simplex?

Project 7.17

Repeat Project 7.16, but increase by one the number of points selected at random in each case.

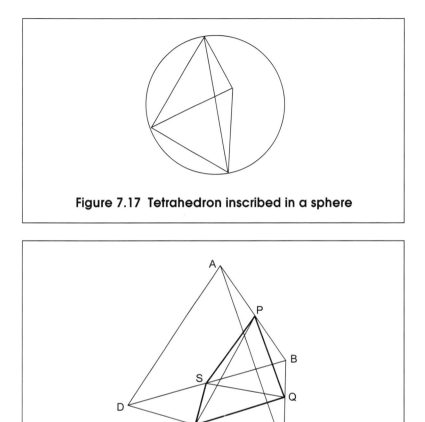

Figure 7.17 Tetrahedron inscribed in a sphere

Figure 7.18 Simplex inscribed in a simplex

Project 7.18

Let ABCD be a simplex in 3-dimensional space and P, Q, R, and S randomly chosen points on ABCD's edges, as in Figure 7.18. Investigate the distribution of volumes of PQRS. Then do the same for P, Q, R, and S randomly positioned on ABCD's faces.

GEOMETRIC MODELS

Project 7.19
Visual models of algebraic and number theory identities are valuable as teaching tools and memory aids. Figures 7.19–7.22 show the visual models of the following familiar identities:

7.19: $(a + b)^2 = a^2 + 2ab + b^2$
7.20: $a^2 - b^2 = (a - b)(a + b)$
7.21: $1 + 3 + 5 + \ldots + (2n - 1) = n^2$
7.22: $1 + 2 + 3 + \ldots + n = n(n + 1)/2$

There are many other identities that students encounter in high school and college mathematics such as

$$(a + b + c)^2 = a^2 + b^2 + c^2 + 2ab + 2ac + 2bc$$

or

$$1^2 + 2^2 + \ldots + n^2 = n(n + 1)(2n + 1)/6$$

or

$$1^3 + 2^3 + \ldots + n^3 = (1 + 2 + \ldots + n)^2$$

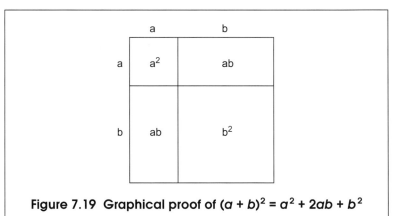

Figure 7.19 Graphical proof of $(a + b)^2 = a^2 + 2ab + b^2$

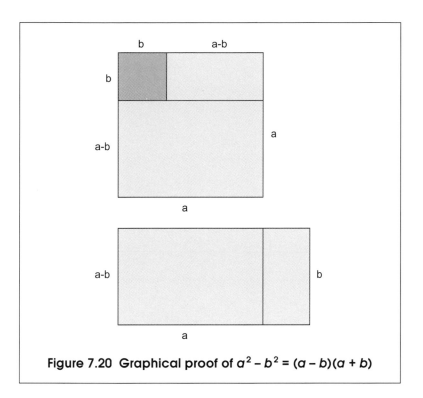

Figure 7.20 Graphical proof of $a^2 - b^2 = (a - b)(a + b)$

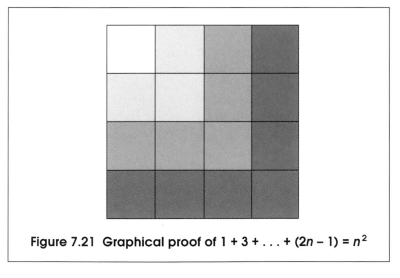

Figure 7.21 Graphical proof of $1 + 3 + \ldots + (2n - 1) = n^2$

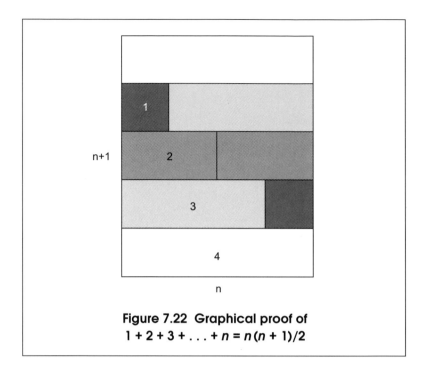

Figure 7.22 Graphical proof of
$1 + 2 + 3 + \ldots + n = n(n + 1)/2$

Develop geometrical models (2- or 3-dimensional as need-ed) for these and other identities.

Project 7.20
Most high school students are unaware of the existence of non-Euclidean geometries. A study of even one of these non-Euclidean geometries is certain to lead to interesting and even startling results for students who have always believed that Euclid had all the answers.

The first non-Euclidean geometry, discovered in the nine-teenth century by the Russian mathematician Nikolay Lobachevsky, is generally known as hyperbolic geometry. Like Euclidean geometry, hyperbolic geometry is based on five postulates. In fact, Euclidean and hyperbolic geometry have the same first four postulates:

- There is exactly one line through any pair of points.
- Any line segment with given endpoints may be extended indefinitely in either direction.
- It is possible to construct a circle with any center and any radius.
- All right angles are congruent.

The fifth postulate is different, however. Euclidean geometry states:

- Given a line L and a point P not on L, there is exactly one line parallel to L through P.
- In hyperbolic geometry, the fifth postulate states:
- Given a line L and a point P not on L, there are at least two distinct lines parallel to L through P.

Visualizing any geometry in which the hyperbolic postulate could be true is difficult. Fortunately, an easy-to-use computer model of hyperbolic geometry is available for Macintosh computers. The name of the software is NonEuclid (see Chapter 8).

NonEuclid is based on French mathematician Jules-Henri Poincaré's model of hyperbolic geometry. He defined the hyperbolic universe as being contained within a Euclidean circle, as shown in Figure 7.23. In this space, rulers shrink (distances grow larger) as they approach the circle so that, from the viewpoint of an inhabitant, the universe is infinite. As a result, the shortest distance between points sometimes falls on arcs of circles orthogonal to the bounding circle of the model.

In other words, in this model, "straight" lines are sometimes what we call "curves" in Euclidean space. This leads to some interesting consequences. For example, note that the sum of the angles of triangle ABC is less than 180. Also, note that the center of circle D appears offset from a Euclidean point of view.

Investigate the following topics in hyperbolic space using NonEuclid and your high school geometry book as a guide.

- Linear and angular measure.
- Congruent triangles. Do they always look the same?

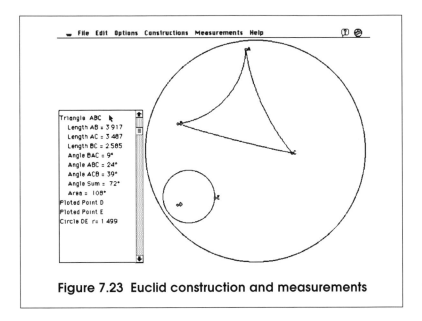

Figure 7.23 Euclid construction and measurements

• Can hyperbolic space be tiled in the same sense as Euclidean space?

• Area. What would you use as the standard unit of area?

• Is analytic (coordinate) geometry possible in hyperbolic space?

Project 7.21

Focusing on the differences between Euclidean space and hyperbolic space, write a science-fiction story about astronauts who go to another universe where the geometry is hyperbolic.

Project 7.22

The geometry that cosmologists use to study the universe is called Minkowski geometry, in honor of the German mathematician Hermann Minkowski. Develop a 2-dimensional model of Minkowski space showing the curvature of space-time and other strange effects of the interaction of matter and space.

FRACTAL GEOMETRY

Another type of geometry currently attracting a lot of attention is fractal geometry, which as we saw in Chapter 3 is the geometry of nature. With commonly available computer equipment and software packages, it is easy to get started in this interesting field.

This is a frame from an abstract animation created with a fractal-based process by Brian Evans at the National Center for Supercomputing Applications. He used the same mathematical algorithm to generate the musical score that accompanied the animation.

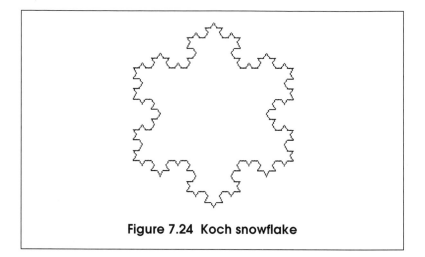

Figure 7.24 Koch snowflake

Project 7.23

One of the first fractal objects investigated by students is the von Koch snowflake curve, which is shown in Figure 7.24. This curve may be generated by using any version of the Logo computer language. You may observe the development of the snowflake curve with the following program, which is written in LogoWriter.

PROGRAM LISTING 1

```
TO DO :N
START
REPEAT 3[IFELSE :N = 0 [FD :L] [LINE :N] RT 120]
END
TO START
MAKE "X 1
REPEAT :N[MAKE "X 3 * :X]
MAKE "L 162 / :X
RG PU HT RT 60 BK 90 LT 30 PD
END
TO LINE :Y
```

```
IFELSE :Y = 1 [SMALLEST] [STEPDOWN]
END
TO SMALLEST
FD :L LT 60 FD :L RT 120 FD :L LT 60 FD :L
END
TO STEPDOWN
LINE :Y – 1 LT 60 LINE :Y – 1 RT 120 LINE :Y – 1 LT 60 LINE :Y – 1
END
```

To see each stage of the snowflake development beginning with an equilateral triangle, type the series of commands DO 0, DO 1, DO 2, DO 3, DO 4, and so on. Then consider the following questions:

• As we increase the number of iterations, or levels at which the object's "theme" is expressed, what happens to the perimeter of the object?

• What happens to the area of the object?

• If you could DO ∞what would the perimeter be? What would the area be?

These and other questions may be answered by systematically collecting and analyzing data as follows:

• First count the number of segments at each "level" and record the data in a table:

N	# OF SEGMENTS, s		
0	3	=	3
1	$4(3)$	=	12
2	$4^2(3)$	=	48
3	$4^3(3)$	=	192
n	$4^n(3)$		

• Next observe that the length of each segment may be written as $\frac{L}{3^n}$, where L is the length of the side of the original equilateral triangle.

• You may then write the perimeter of the curve as (# segments)(segment length) = $(4^n(3))(\frac{L}{3^n}) = 3L(\frac{4}{3})^n = P_o(\frac{4}{3})^n$, where P_o is the perimeter of the original equilateral triangle. Clearly, as n increases without bound, the perimeter does the same. This is an example of a divergent geometric sequence.

To find out what happens to the area, take a similar approach as follows:

• Create a table of data based on the triangular areas shown in Figure 7.25. Assume the big triangle has an area of 1.

N	S	# TRIANGLES ADDED = # OF SEGMENTS AT THE PREVIOUS LEVEL	ADDITIONAL AREA
0	3		
1	12	3	$3(\frac{1}{9})$
2	48	12	$12(\frac{1}{9})^2$
3	192	48	$48(\frac{1}{9})^3$
n	$4^n(3)$	$4^{n-1}(3)$	$4^{n-1}(3)(\frac{1}{9})^n$

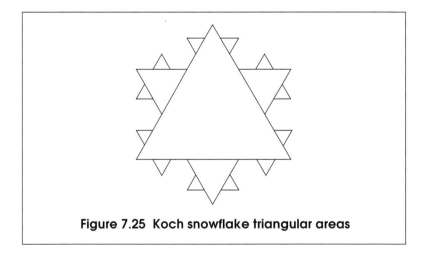

Figure 7.25 Koch snowflake triangular areas

If the original equilateral triangle has an area of 1, the area for the curve on the nth iteration is

$$1 + \sum_{i=1}^{n} 4^{i-1}(3)(\tfrac{1}{9})^i = 1 + \tfrac{1}{3}\sum_{i=1}^{n}(\tfrac{4}{9})^{i-1}$$

which, as n goes to infinity, is a convergent geometric series with sum 1.6.

To summarize the findings, the von Koch curve in its limiting case has an infinite perimeter but a finite area.

Study each of the following computer programs until you understand how it works. Each generates a different fractal curve. Investigate each curve with the goal of developing expressions for the perimeter and the enclosed area for any value of n in the expression DO n.

PROGRAM LISTING 2

```
START
REPEAT 3[IFELSE :N = 0 [FD :L] [LINE :N] RT 120]
END
TO START
MAKE "X 1
REPEAT :N[MAKE "X 3 * :X]
MAKE "L 162 / :X
RG PU HT RT 60 BK 90 LT 30 PD
END
TO LINE :Y
IFELSE :Y = 1 [SMALLEST] [STEPDOWN]
END
TO SMALLEST
FD :L RT 60 FD :L LT 120 FD :L RT 60 FD :L
END
TO STEPDOWN
LINE :Y − 1 RT 60 LINE :Y − 1 LT 120 LINE :Y − 1 RT 60 LINE :Y − 1
END
```

```
TO DO :N
START
REPEAT 3[IFELSE :N=0 [FD :L] [LINE :N] RT 120]
END
TO START
MAKE "X 1
REPEAT :N[MAKE "X 4 * :X]
MAKE "L 108 / :X
RG PU HT RT 60 BK 50 LT 30 PD
END
TO LINE :Y
IFELSE :Y = 1 [SMALLEST] [STEPDOWN]
END
TO SMALLEST
FD :L LT 90 FD :L RT 90 FD :L RT 90 FD :L FD :L
LT 90 FD :L LT 90 FD :L RT 90 FD :L
END
TO STEPDOWN
LINE :Y – 1 LT 90 LINE :Y – 1 RT 90 LINE :Y – 1 RT 90 LINE :Y – 1
LINE :Y – 1 LT 90 LINE :Y – 1 LT 90 LINE :Y – 1 RT 90 LINE :Y – 1
END
```

Project 7.24

The Logo program on the following page will show you the
iterations of the Sierpinski gasket, which was introduced in
Chapter 3. This fractal is interesting because its fractal nature
lies in its interior rather than along its boundary.

Figure 7.26 shows the first three iterations produced by
the program. The process starts with the triangle (instead of a
unit square as in Chapter 3) in the upper left-hand corner of
the figure. On the next iteration, the triangle is divided into
three smaller versions of itself. Then it is divided into nine smaller versions of itself with similar empty spaces in between.

```
TO DO :N
RG HT
PU SETPOS [−100 120] PD
EXP2 :N
MAKE "S 160 / :X
IFELSE :N > 0 [TRIBOX :N]
[FD 160 RT 90 FD 160 RT 135 FD 160 * 1.4142 RT 135 PU FD
15 RT 90 FD 5 PD FILL]
END
TO EXP2 :N
MAKE "X 1
REPEAT :N[MAKE "X 2 * :X]
END
TO BOX :N
REPEAT 2[FD :S RT 90]
RT 45 FD :S * 1.4142 RT 160
PU FD 3 PD FILL PU BK 3 LT 25 PD
END
TO TRIBOX :N
IFELSE :N = 1 [BOX :N FD :S BOX :N RT 90 FD :S LT 90
BOX :N RT 45 BK :S * 1.4142 LT 45]
[MAKE "X :X / 2 TRIBOX :N − 1 FD :S * :X TRIBOX :N − 1 RT 90
FD :S * :X LT 90 TRIBOX :N − 1 RT 45 BK :S * 1.4142 * :X LT 45
MAKE "X :X * 2]
END
```

As before, determine the total perimeter and area of the shaded regions at each step in the development of the fractal. Express your findings in appropriate mathematical notation.

Then modify the program so that the object is constructed of squares, as shown in Figure 7.27. What changes, if any, do you find in the limiting case, where $n = \infty$ in the expression DO n?

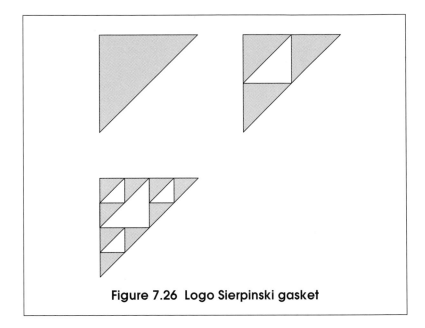

Figure 7.26 Logo Sierpinski gasket

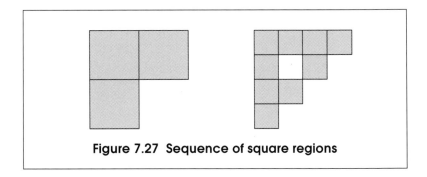

Figure 7.27 Sequence of square regions

Project 7.25
Two intersecting circles are orthogonal if the tangents drawn to each curve at their points of intersection are perpendicular. The two smaller circles in Figure 7.28 are orthogonal to

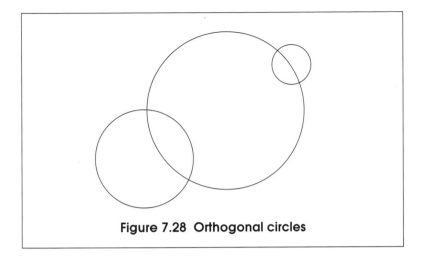

Figure 7.28 Orthogonal circles

the larger circles, as you can see if you draw two tangents at each intersection.

Create a computer program that will draw arcs orthogonal to a circle, given two points on the arc. Extend this procedure to 3-space, creating orthogonal spheres.

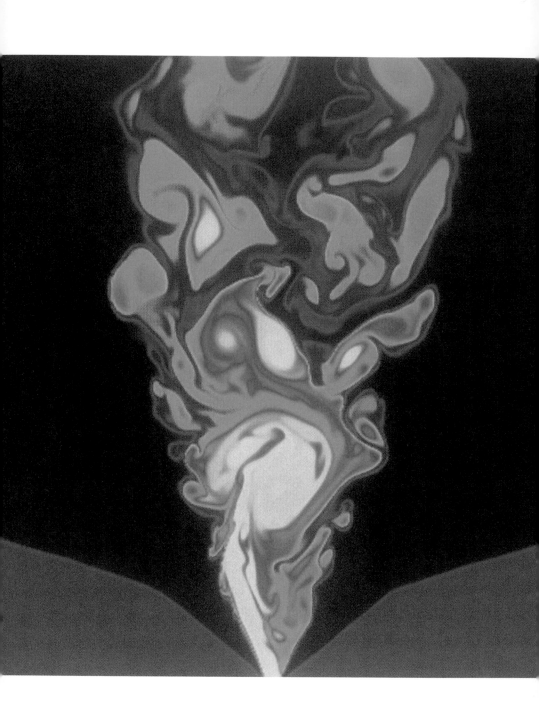

8

COMPUTER TOOLS
FOR VISUALIZATION

The geometries discussed in preceding chapters cannot be fully appreciated unless you can visualize them. Recently developed computer packages are invaluable for this purpose.

NONEUCLID

Non-Euclidean geometries are rarely even mentioned in high-school mathematics. As a result, most high school students believe Euclid's is the only geometry. And students interested in exploring alternative geometries frequently discover that there are no books or computer programs readily available to guide them. There is one notable exception to this generally sad state of affairs: hyperbolic, or Lobachevskian, geometry.

For exploring hyperbolic geometry, it is hard to beat the computer microworld called NonEuclid. Available for Macintosh computers, the program is a microworld of Poincaré's model of hyperbolic geometry. Points, lines, triangles, and other objects are created by using a simple menu system. Measurements are made the same way. A sample construction and measurement screen created by NonEuclid is shown in Figure 7.23.

For information on how to obtain NonEuclid by anonymous file transfer over e-mail (softlib@cs.rice.edu) or by regular mail, contact Danny Powell, CITI/CRPC, Rice University, Houston, TX 77251.

FRACTINT

FRACTINT is the best of the free fractal geometry programs for IBM-compatible personal computers. It will help you visualize fractals, which are discussed in Chapters 3 and 7. The program is fast, easy to use, and very versatile. That versatility may be seen in the following partial list of topics taken from the FRACTINT documentation:

"3D" Images
Barnsley IFS Fractals
Barnsley Mandelbrot/Julia Sets
Bifurcation
Biomorphs
Complex Newton
Continuous Potential
Diffusion Limited Aggregation
Distance Estimator
Fractal Types
Gingerbreadman
Henon Attractors
Julia Sets
Julibrots
Kam Torus
L-Systems
Lambda Sets
Lambdafn
Lorenz Attractors

Lyapunov Fractals
Magnetic Fractals
Mandelbrot Set
Mandelfn
Mandellambda Sets
Martin Attractors
Newton
Newton Domains of Attraction
Orbit Fractals
Peterson Variations
Pickover Attractors
Pickover Popcorn
Pickover Mandelbrot/Julia Types
Plasma Clouds
Quartic Mandelbrot/Julia
Rossler Attractors
Scott Taylor/Lee Skinner Variations
Sierpinski Gasket
Starfields

The package is in constant revision, and new versions may be obtained from software distribution services, electronic mail bulletin boards and file servers, and local computer clubs. New versions of FRACTINT are originally posted to the CompuServe network in the "Fractals" library of the COMART forum in the form of two self-extracting archive files—FRAINT.EXE (executable & documentation) and FRASRC.EXE (source code). Information on CompuServe and its graphics forums can be obtained by calling (800) 848-8199. Ask for operator number 229. If you don't have access to CompuServe, many other sites tend to carry these files shortly after their initial release, although sometimes under different names.

If you have access to the Internet, FRACTINT is available through SIMTEL20 and its various mirror sites. Look in the PD:<MSDOS.GRAPHICS> directory for files named FRA*.*. If you have a modem, a number of computer bulletin boards carry the latest version of FRACTINT. The "Ideal Studies BBS" (508)757-1806, 1200/2400/9600HST is one such BBS. If you don't have a modem, Public (Software) Library, PO Box 35705, Houston, TX 77235-5705, USA, phone (800) 242-4775, will ship you diskettes containing the latest versions of FRACTINT for a nominal fee.

SCIENTIFIC VISUALIZATION TOOLS

One of the long-term effects of current reforms in science and mathematics education will be a greater integration of science and mathematics content. The real impetus for this change is a shift in emphasis in school science and mathematics from the facts to the processes of science and mathematics.

To students, that shift will mean spending more time investigating ideas directly and less time reading about other people's investigations. In this approach, students will ask meaningful mathematical and scientific questions, obtain data from a variety of sources, analyze data by using appropriate mathematical procedures and computational tools, and reach their own conclusions.

Many high school students regularly analyze 2-dimensional data sets by graphing them on a calculator or computer. One of the variables is designated the independent variable, x, and the other is designated the dependent variable, $f(x)$, or y. The dependent variable is then graphed as a function of the independent variable. Many computer graphing packages and graphing calculators are available for this type of analysis.

When 3-dimensional data must be analyzed, however, the situation is very different. There are very few computer programs for high-school students that graph functions of two variables. This is unfortunate since many interesting scientific questions involve 3-dimensional data sets. For instance, satellite images of Earth and the other planets of our solar system are created with 3-dimensional data sets.

**A supercomputer created this 3-dimensional
image of Maat Mons on Venus from radar data
supplied by the Magellan space probe.**

In these data sets, each location on the surface requires
two parameters or coordinates (*x-y*, or longitude-latitude).
Associated with each location is a third parameter that characterizes some feature of the planet (cloud cover, temperature, ozone layer overhead, radiated/reflected energy, and
so on) at that location. Representing such data sets in graphical form requires sophisticated computer software. The

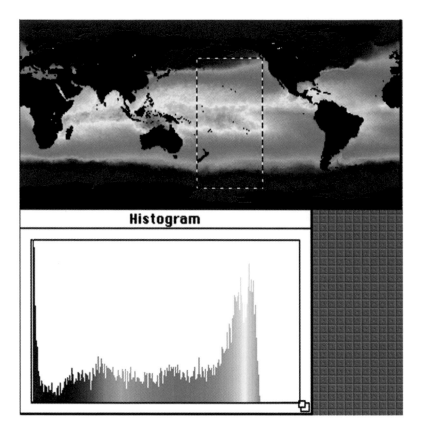

**This map, which indicates ocean temperatures
by color, was generated on a personal computer.**

process of rendering realistic images with 3(or more)-dimen-
sional data sets is often called scientific visualization.

A new generation of scientific visualization tools is now
being developed for both scientists and students. One of
the best sources of these programs is the National Center
for Supercomputing Applications (NCSA), 605 East Springfield Avenue, University of Illinois at Urbana-Champaign,
Champaign, IL 61820-5518, phone (217) 244-4130. In addition to its role as a supercomputing research center, NCSA

develops and distributes scientific visualization software for PCs, Macintosh computers, and Unix-based graphics work-stations.

Information on NCSA products and services is summarized in NCSA's Technical Resources Catalog, available free of charge. NCSA also publishes an educational magazine in video format on scientific computing called *Real Time*; a magazine called *Access* (free of charge) focusing on the various projects directed by NCSA; CD-ROMs of scientific images and data sets; software documentation and updates; and preprints of scientific articles involving high performance computing and NCSA personnel. All of NCSA's products are either free or low-cost (typically $5 – $30). NCSA has an educational mission specifically aimed at involving high school teachers and students in high performance computing, so interested students and teachers should not hesitate to contact NCSA for assistance.

Among the many products offered by NCSA, the following are particularly useful in analyzing 3-dimensional data sets:

• NCSA Collage. The newest NCSA software release is both a scientific visualization tool and a conferencing tool. Data may be visualized and shared simultaneously by a group of users, all having access to the Internet.

• NCSA DataScope. Data is placed in a spreadsheet format and may be transformed using FORTRAN-like commands. Color raster graphic images, like the one shown in Figure 8.1, may be generated from each data set.

• NCSA Image. Data may be represented in a variety of image formats including color raster graphic, contour plots, and mesh (wire-frame) diagrams like the one in Figure 8.2. By manipulating the color palette associated with each image, various features may be emphasized or de-emphasized. Statistical analyses may be performed and histograms plotted. Multiple image sets may be animated to produce movies of scientific processes.

• NCSA Layout. A tool for creating finished, presentation-quality slides: labels, legends, and so on.

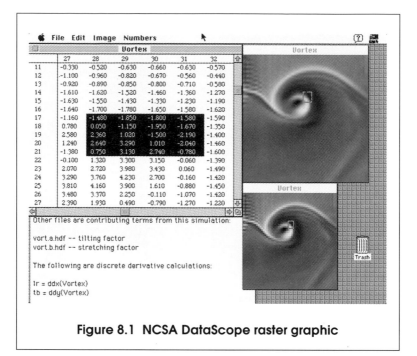

Figure 8.1 NCSA DataScope raster graphic

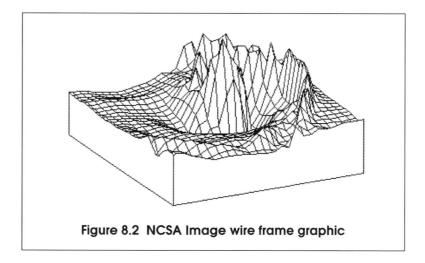

Figure 8.2 NCSA Image wire frame graphic

• NCSA PalEdit. A tool for creating custom color palettes.

These and other NCSA computer software packages—and documentation for them—are available to users on the Internet computer network. Invoke the file transfer protocol at your local Internet host by typing

ftp ftp.ncsa.uiuc.edu

Log onto the NCSA server as anonymous and use your Internet address as the password. Next, enter

get README.FIRST

to transfer the instructions on how to proceed to your local Internet host.

Finally, NCSA has a Media Services Department that can turn your computer graphics into 35-millimeter slides, overhead transparencies, or VHS format animations. This service makes it possible for student researchers to share their findings in a dramatic fashion at science fairs and other forums. Inquiries may be sent via the Internet to media@ncsa. uiuc.edu.

SCIENTIFIC DATA SETS ON CD-ROM

It is not enough to have an easy-to-use scientific visualization software tool. Students and teachers need interesting scientific data sets that they can use to practice their visualization skills and that prompt them to ask meaningful scientific questions. Fortunately, NASA has already filled this need in CD-ROMs available from the National Space Science Data Center, NASA/Goddard Space Flight Center, Code 633, Greenbelt, MD 20771. You may contact the center for a catalog of CD-ROMs by mail, by phone (301) 286-6695, by fax (301) 286-4952, or via the Internet at request@nssdca.gsfc. nasa.gov. A sample of available titles follows:

• Einstein Observatory CD-ROMs. Thirteen disks containing images of astronomical X-ray sources.

• Geologic Remote Sensing Field Experiment. Nine disks with aircraft and field images of California and Nevada.

• The Greenhouse Effect Detection Experiment (GEDEX). Includes PC viewing software.

• International Halley Watch. Twenty-three disks.

• IRAS Sky Survey Atlas. Four disks of infrared astronomical images.

• Magellan (MIDR). Fifty-two disks of Venus.

• Mosaicked Digital Image Models. Six disks of Mars.

• Toms Ozone Image Data Update. One disk covering November 1979 January 1992.

• Voyager Spacecraft to the Outer Planets. Twelve disks.

• Viking Orbiter Images of Mars. Eight disks.

Many other CD-ROM data and image sets are available from other sources. For example, the following titles are taken from a catalog of CD-ROMs available from NASA Ames Research Center, Mail Stop 245-5, Moffett Field, CA 94035-1000, phone (415) 604-5076, Internet HIPSKIND@HECTOR.ARC.NASA.GOV.

• The Airborne Antarctic Ozone Experiment (AAOE).

• The Airborne Arctic Stratospheric Expedition (AASE) and the Meteorological Measurement System (MMS).

• The Stratosphere-Troposphere Exchange Project (STEP).

From the NASA Jet Propulsion Laboratory, Mail Stop 300-323, California Institute of Technology, Pasadena, CA 91109, phone (818) 354-5327, you can get:

• Tropical Ocean Global Atmosphere (TOGA) Meteorological and Oceanographic Data Sets for 1985 and 1986.

From the National Snow and Ice Data Center, CIRES, Campus Box 449, University of Colorado at Boulder, CO 80309, phone (303) 492-1834, Internet HANSON@KYROS.COLORADO.EDU :

• A Global Ecosystems Database developed by the Environmental Protection Agency (EPA) and the National Oceanic Atmospheric Administration (NOAA).

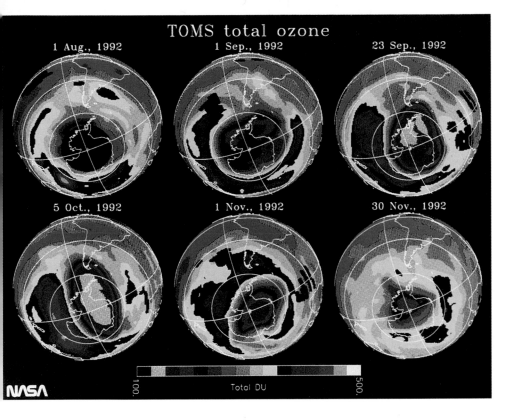

TOMS total ozone

1 Aug., 1992   1 Sep., 1992   23 Sep., 1992

5 Oct., 1992   1 Nov., 1992   30 Nov., 1992

Total DU

These maps showing global ozone concentrations were created from the Toms Ozone data set. Reds and greens indicate
high ozone concentrations, while blues and purples indicate
low concentrations. Data were unavailable for the black areas.

- Geophysics of North America.
- Land Gravity Data Base.

Thus, students interested in mathematics projects involving
statistical analysis or mathematical modeling of real world
data now have access to many interesting data sets as well
as scientific visualization software. When NASA's Mission to
Planet Earth satellite system begins beaming a gigabyte of
data per second back to Earth, it will be possible for students
to "grab" images of their own geographical areas off the

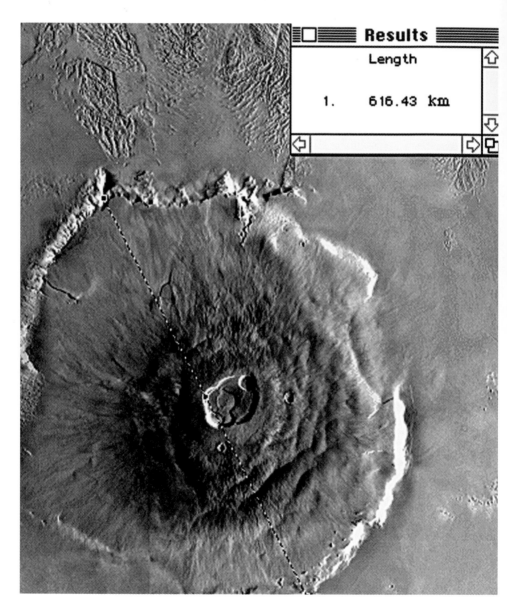

Results

Length

1.   616.43 km

The image of Olympus Mons, on Mars, was
created on a personal computer with software
from the National Institutes of Health.

Internet. Who knows what environmental problems will then be first identified by high school students investigating their own corner of planet Earth?

Project 8.1
Obtain copies of NCSA DataScope, Image, and Collage and use them to examine satellite images of Mars, available from NASA. Are some parts of Mars more heavily cratered than others? Are there more small craters than large craters? Create a histogram showing the distribution of craters by size.

Project 8.2
Using the tools in Project 8.1, examine satellite images of Earth, and determine whether they support the existence of a hole in the Earth's ozone layer.

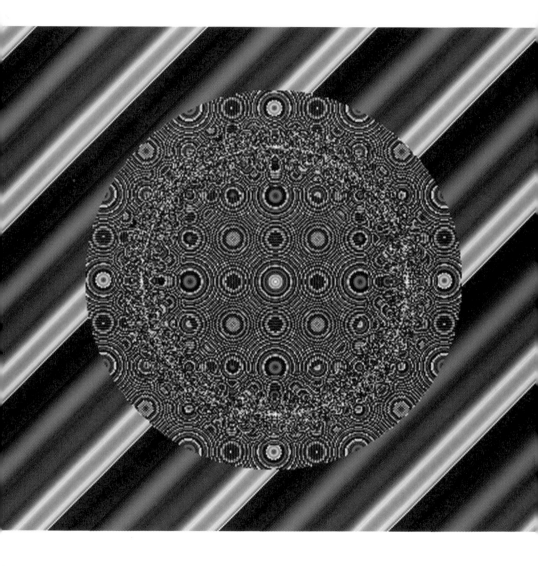

9

NUMBER THEORY

Number theory is a favorite branch of mathematics for students doing research projects, principally because questions concerning divisibility and prime numbers, perfect numbers, and many other topics in number theory often may be grasped immediately, without lengthy background reading. Of course, solving such problems often requires genuine insight and creativity. The following project ideas vary in difficulty, but all offer interesting food for thought.

Project 9.1
Prime numbers are positive integers, n, that have no integral divisors greater than 1, other than themselves. The list of primes begins 2, 3, 5, 7, 11, 13, 17, 19, . . . , and goes on forever. (Can you prove that?)

Many primes are of the form $n^2 + 1$, where n is a natural number. For example, $1^2 + 1 = 2$; $2^2 + 1 = 5$; $4^2 + 1 = 17$; and so on. For which values of n does the expression $n^2 + 1$ produce a prime? Are there an infinite number of such primes?

Project 9.2

Many other primes are of the form $n! + 1$, where n is a natural number. For example, $1! + 1 = 2$; $2! + 1 = 3$; $3! + 1 = 7$; and so on. For which values of n does the expression $n! + 1$ produce a prime? Are there an infinite number of such primes?

Project 9.3

Many primes are of the form $n! - (n-1)! + (n-2)! - \ldots - (-1)^n$, as in the expression $4! - 3! + 2! - 1! = 19$. For which values of n does this type of expression generate a prime? Are there an infinite number of such primes?

Project 9.4

Let n be a positive integer greater than 1 and define $f(n)$ as the number of ways that n may be represented as a sum of two or more consecutive primes. For example, 5 may be expressed as $2 + 3$, so $f(5) = 1$. Also, 41 may be represented as $11 + 13 + 17$ or as $2 + 3 + 5 + 7 + 11 + 13$, so $f(41) = 2$. For some integers, like 3, $f(n) = 0$; that is, there is no way to represent the integer as the sum of two or more consecutive primes. For what numbers is $f(n) > 0$?

Project 9.5

The integer 10 may be represented as the sum of the cubes of four integers: $(3)^3 + (-2)^3 + (-2)^3 + (-1)^3$. Likewise, $3 = (3)^3 + (-2)^3 + (-2)^3 + (-2)^3$. Investigate whether every integer may be represented as the sum of four cubes.

Project 9.6

If $m, n, p,$ and q are primes, under what conditions is it possible to cover an $m \times n$ rectangle with smaller $p \times q$ rectangles in such a way that they do not overlap? (see Figure 9.1)

Project 9.7

A single number sequence may be used to represent the solution of each of the following problems. Solve each problem and find the number sequence.

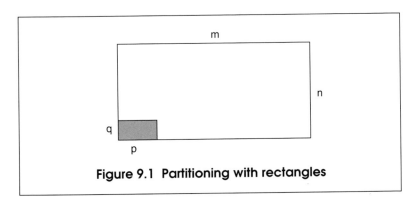

Figure 9.1 Partitioning with rectangles

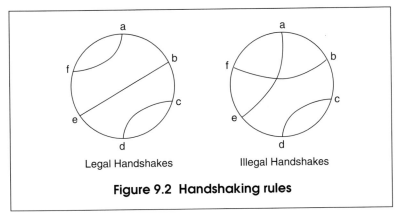

Legal Handshakes   Illegal Handshakes

Figure 9.2 Handshaking rules

• 2*n* people sitting at a round table start shaking hands as follows: Each person turns to the side or reaches across the table to shake a hand, executing a first set of handshakes. In each set, there must be no more than one pair of handshakers who reach across the table (see Figure 9.2). Then a second set of handshakes takes place. This procedure continues until all possible handshakes have occurred. Find a rule for determining the number of handshakes *n* people will make when they follow this procedure.

• Examine Figures 9.3–9.6. Each is a "trunk" with one or more "branches" growing from it. As the figures demonstrate, there is/are:

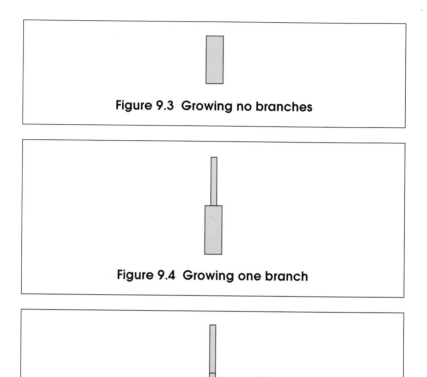

Figure 9.3 Growing no branches

Figure 9.4 Growing one branch

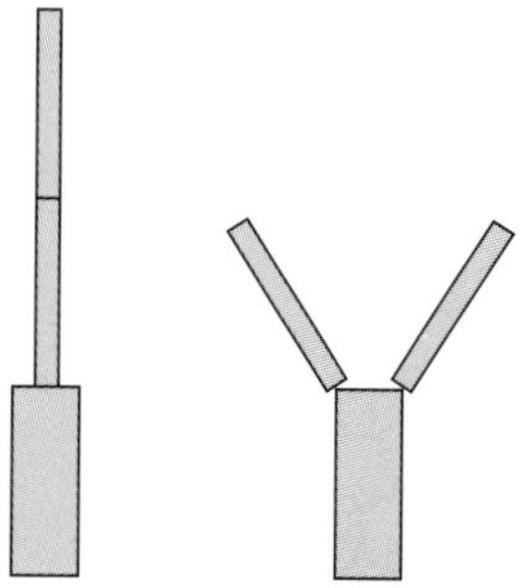

Figure 9.5 Growing two branches

1 way to grow zero branches,
1 way to grow one branch,
2 ways to grow two branches, and
5 ways to grow three branches.
  One convention for representing each configuration relies on the sequence of motions in drawing the branches.

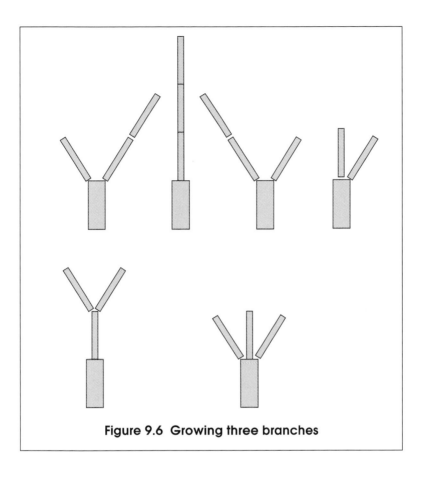

Figure 9.6 Growing three branches

To draw one branch, the pencil moves forward, which we will represent by "(," and then moves back, represented by ")." Two branches can be drawn by moving forward and back twice—"()()"—or to avoid lifting the pencil from the paper, by moving forward twice and then back twice—"(())." Using this convention, each of the figures may be "drawn" as follows:

1 branch: ()
2 branches: ()() or (())
3 branches: ((())) or ()(()) or (())() or (()()) or ()()()
Extend the list by investigating more complex branching

schemes and then develop a mathematical rule for computing the number of configurations for each set of branches.

Project 9.8

In the well-known Tower of Hanoi puzzle, *n* disks stacked on a post as in Figure 9.7 are systematically moved between 3 posts—A, B, and C. The goal is to relocate the original stack from post A to post B or C. The difficulty arises from the stipulation that no larger disk may ever rest above a smaller disk on any of the three posts. The movements of each disk may be recorded as a sequence of letters representing the posts visited by the disk during the game: for disk #1, the sequence might be ABCAB, . . . and so on. You might think of the sequence as a "path" taken by the disk.

• Investigate the path of each of *n* disks in the course of a game in which you try to solve the puzzle in the least number of moves possible. How are the paths of the various disks different? How are they the same?

• Can the path of disk #1 in a "least-number-of-moves" game always be found embedded in its path during less efficient but nevertheless successful games? Of disk #2? Of disk #3?

• Every move involves two posts, leaving one post unused. Examine the sequence of unused posts. How is the path of unused posts like the paths of various disks? How is it different?

• Starting from the game's initial conditions, is it possible to

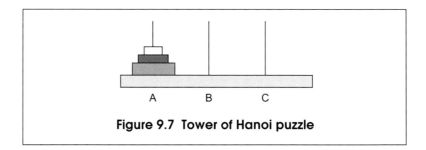

Figure 9.7 Tower of Hanoi puzzle

produce any arrangement of disks on the posts, such as disks #1 and #2 on the first post and disk #3 on the third post (though still never putting larger disks over smaller disks)?

Project 9.9
The Fibonacci sequence of numbers begins 1, 1, 2, 3, 5, 8, 13, 21, 34, 55, . . . and so on. Each element in the list (except the first) is the sum of the two numbers before it.

Many integers can be represented as the sum of smaller Fibonacci numbers. For example, $2 = 1 + 1$, $3 = 2 + 1$, $4 = 3 + 1$, $5 = 3 + 2$, $6 = 5 + 1$, $7 = 5 + 2$, and so on. Is it possible to represent every integer greater than 1 in this manner? If it is possible, is there only one such representation for every integer? If so, write a computer program to express each integer n as a sum of smaller Fibonacci numbers.

Project 9.10
A rhyming square is any square with an area that ends in the same digits as its length. For example:

5*5 = 25, represents a rhyming square of order 1 (one digit is repeated);

25*25 = 625, an order 2 rhyming square; and

76*76 = 5776, also an order 2 rhyming square.

Can a rhyming square be found of any length n, where n is a positive integer? Write a computer program for finding all the rhyming squares of a given order.

Project 9.11
Follow the same general instructions as in Project 9.10 operating in some other number base, such as base 7 or base 8. Are rhyming squares more common in some bases than others?

Project 9.12
Model a game in which one player chooses an integer k from the closed interval $(1, n)$, where n is a natural number greater

than 1. The second player tries to guess k, given n. If the second player's guess, m, is less than k, he pays the first player \$1; otherwise he pays \$2. The second player continues guessing and paying in this manner until he discovers k. How should the second player select his guesses in order to minimize his payments?

Project 9.13
A complex number $a + bi$ is called Gaussian if both its real and imaginary parts are integers, that is, if a and b are integers. A Gaussian number is called prime if it cannot be represented as a product of two Gaussian numbers different from 1, -1, i, and -i. For example, $2 = (1 + i) * (1 - i)$ is not prime, but $2 + i$ is prime.

Write a computer program for determining whether a given Gaussian number is prime and for representing a given Gaussian number as a product of Gaussian primes.

Project 9.14
A palindromic number is a number that reads the same forward or backward; examples are 1991 or 232 or 4334. There are nine one-digit palindromic numbers: 1, 2, 3, 4, 5, 6, 7, 8, 9. How many two-digit palindromic numbers are there? How many three-digit palindromic numbers? How many n-digit palindromic numbers? How many palindromic numbers are less than 100? Less than 1000? Less than 1,000,000? Less than 10^n?

Project 9.15
Investigate whether it is possible to represent any palindromic number as a sum of smaller palindromic numbers. In addition, investigate whether it is possible to find more than one such sum for any given palindromic number.

Project 9.16
Triangular inequality numbers are sets of three integers corresponding to the lengths of the sides of a triangle. For exam-

ple, (7, 7, 7) are triangular inequality numbers corresponding to the sides of an equilateral triangle; (2, 3, 4) correspond to the sides of a scalene triangle; and (3, 4, 5) correspond to the sides of a right triangle. They are called *inequality* numbers because they must conform to the inequality $a + b > c$; that is, the sum of any two sides of a triangle is always greater than the third side. For example, (1, 2, 3) do not correspond to any triangle.

How many triangular inequality numbers may be formed from a given set of n consecutive integers? Given that n is either even or odd, find the number of scalene, isosceles, and equilateral triangles that can be formed, as well as the total number of triangles.

Project 9.17

A narcissistic number is an integer that is equivalent to some mathematical expression of its digits. For instance, $27 = (\sqrt{2+7})^3$ or $39 = (3!)^2 + \sqrt{9}$. Note that the digits in the expression must retain the order of the digits in the narcissistic number. Investigate whether every positive integer is narcissistic.

Project 9.18

Define the expression 21 (mod 5) to mean the remainder obtained when 21 is divided by 5. The expression 21 (mod 5) $\equiv$ 1 is read "twenty-one mod 5 is congruent to 1." This concept may be extended to include algebraic expressions such as x (mod 5), where x is any whole number. In this sense "mod," which is an abbreviation for "modulus," can be thought of as an operator like multiplication or division. Expressions containing it can be graphed as shown in Figure 9.8. The height of the graph is determined by the size of the modulus, in this case 5; choosing a larger modulus produces a higher graph—that is, the sawtooth curve has longer teeth.

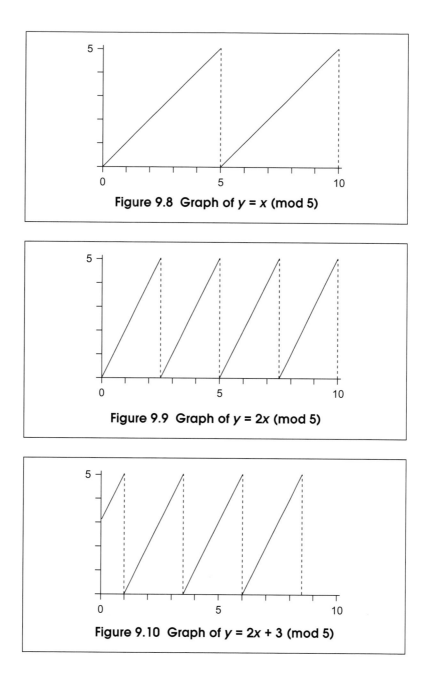

Figure 9.8 Graph of $y = x$ (mod 5)

Figure 9.9 Graph of $y = 2x$ (mod 5)

Figure 9.10 Graph of $y = 2x + 3$ (mod 5)

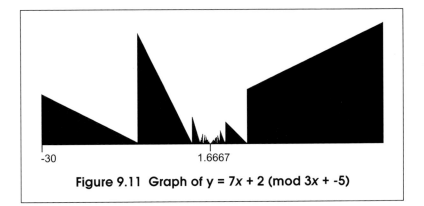

-30   1.6667

Figure 9.11 Graph of y = 7x + 2 (mod 3x + -5)

The expression 2x (mod 5) is graphed in Figure 9.9. Multiplying the variable x by 2 has the effect of shortening the base of each tooth by half, similar to the effect observed when graphing the trigonometric functions: doubling the coefficient of the angle halves the period of the wave. In general, the graph of the expression Ax (mod C) will be a sawtooth curve with period $\frac{C}{A}$ and amplitude C.

Finally, as with the trigonometric functions, the introduction of a constant B in the expression Ax + B (mod C) produces a phase shift in the graph of Ax (mod C). Figure 9.10 illustrates the effect for the graph of 2x + 3 (mod 5). In general, the amount of phase shift is given by $\frac{B}{A}$.

It is possible to consider more complicated expressions such as Ax + B (mod Cx + D), in which the modulus of the expression is not constant but is itself a function of x. Graphically, this results in teeth of varying width and height. Figure 9.11 is the graph of the expression 7x + 2 (mod 3x + -5).

Determine for which values of x the expression in Figure 9.11 is equal to zero. Does each tooth have a straight line for its downward slope? If so, does each tooth have its own unique downward slope? Describe the curve connecting the peaks of all the teeth. Where is the graph continuous? Where are its discontinuities?

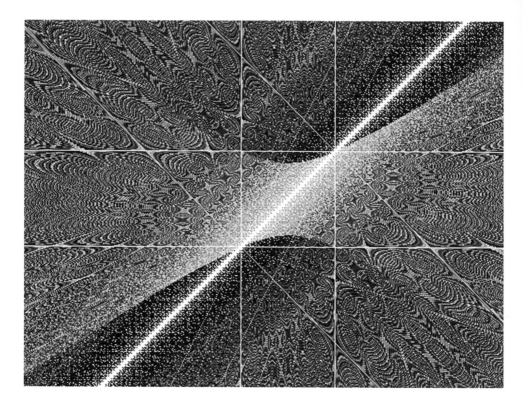

Modulus expressions can create mesmerizing patterns like the one shown here.

Project 9.19

Following the general procedure of Project 9.18, investigate the graphs of quadratic functions such as $x^2 - 40,000$ (mod $\sqrt{x^2 - 20,500}$), which is graphed in Figure 9.12. Graph these functions with the appropriate computer software.

Project 9.20

Following the same general procedure of Project 9.18, investigate the graphs of quadratic functions of two variables, such as $x^2 + y^2 - 40,000$ (mod $\sqrt{x^2 + y^2 - 20,500}$), which is

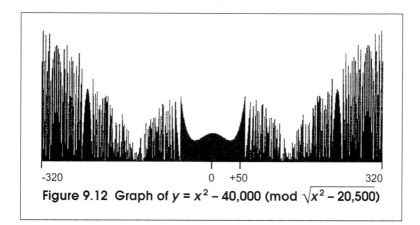

-320   0   +50   320

Figure 9.12 Graph of $y = x^2 - 40,000 \pmod{\sqrt{x^2 - 20,500}}$

graphed in Figure 9.13. Write a computer program that computes $f(x, y)$ for an array of points. Then import that array into a scientific visualization software package such as NCSA DataScope or NCSA Image to graph the results.

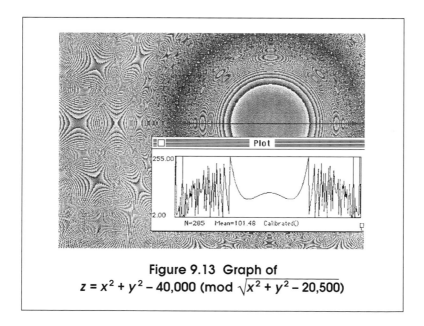

Figure 9.13 Graph of
$$z = x^2 + y^2 - 40,000 \pmod{\sqrt{x^2 + y^2 - 20,500}}$$

POSTSCRIPT
HOW THIS BOOK WAS WRITTEN

My hope is that *Math Projects in the Computer Age* will help students decide whether they want to become mathematicians. To that end, I will tell the story of how the book came to be published and, in so doing, open a window on a side of mathematicians' lives that would surprise most people. Far from the dull and isolated existence that much of the general public assumes, the life of a mathematician can be exciting and wonderful.

The mathematics culture is international, self-sustaining, vital, and eager to welcome new talent. If you decide to become a mathematician, you will be doing more than choosing a career, you will be joining us, the people of this and many other mathematics books, in our international community of scholars. We're waiting for you!

PEOPLE, PLACES, AND PROJECTS

In the spring of 1992, I received a letter from Thomas Cohn, a senior editor at Franklin Watts, inviting me to write a sequel to my 1988 book *Math Projects for Young Scientists*. Since part of my job description as a university mathematics educator is to create new knowledge and educational resources, I found the invitation appealing and began work on a chapter-by-chapter outline. Shortly thereafter, I traveled to Houston, Texas, to present a paper at a conference on educational technologies. While there, I met Dr. Alexei Semenov, director of the Institute of New Technologies (INT) in Moscow, Russia. Over breakfast one morning, Alexei told me an amazing story.

In November of 1989 Vaclav Havel and his democratic reformers staged their "Velvet Revolution," occupying government headquarters in Prague and announcing the end of Communist rule in Czechoslovakia. During the first days of the revolution, while tensions were still high and the outcome in doubt, one of Havel's associates, Dr. Jana Ryslinkova—a mathematician—phoned Alexei Semenov in Moscow and asked him to fly to Prague and to bring the fax machine from his office.

This he did, and for the next several weeks, he and his teenage daughter worked the fax machine night and day, aiding the reformers in getting official recognition for their new government from the United Nations, their European neighbors, the United States, and other governments.

When I met Alexei in 1992, he and Jana were traveling in the United States on a prestigious Eisenhower Fellowship, which was granted in recognition of their outstanding service in the interest of democratic ideals. As a member of Czechoslovakia's first democratically elected parliament, Jana was studying American government as well as meeting with mathematicians and mathematics educators. Alexei was looking for meaningful collaborative activities with American universities and publishers of educational materials.

When I described my interest in developing a sequel to *Math Projects for Young Scientists*, he immediately made a number of suggestions concerning the content and organization of the proposed book. We both started thinking about some sort of collaboration.

Over the next two months, I met with Alexei and Jana two more times to develop an understanding of what Alexei and his associates at INT might contribute to this book and how I would pay them for their assistance. The day we reached our final agreement, we celebrated by driving the 90 miles from my home in Bozeman, Montana, to Yellowstone National Park. There we relaxed in a natural hot spring high in the mountains, a herd of elk grazing only a few yards from our steaming "hot pot." For the man from Moscow, it might as well have been another planet.

Shortly after leaving Bozeman, Alexei returned to Moscow. Using electronic mail, we continued our correspondence and he and his associates sent me project ideas and described projects currently under way in the Moscow public schools, particularly Moscow School # 57. Soon, I was exchanging e-mail messages with a number of people. Their names fascinated me: Sergei, Sasha, Elena, and many more. So eager, so friendly, so far away.

Back home at Montana State University, two of my graduate students, Kate Riley and Tod Shockey, were beginning background research for the book and trying their hands at writing project ideas. So, with contributions from mathematics educators on two continents, the book began to develop.

A VISIT TO MOSCOW

On December 11, 1992, my wife and daughter and I flew to Moscow. For the next three weeks, I worked with Alexei and other INT personnel on project ideas and the beginnings of a manuscript. What fun it was finally to meet the mathematicians whom for months I could only know as e-mail correspondents!

They turned out to be generous, friendly, talented people with beautiful families who opened their homes and their hearts to us.

During our many meetings and work sessions, three things happened. First, the book began to take shape. Second, we became friends. Third, we began thinking about new ways that we could collaborate and help one another.

BACK HOME

Back in the United States, I continued researching and writing. When the manuscript was completed in June of 1993, I mailed it to Thomas Cohn at Franklin Watts. There, a team of editors and book makers began their work on the manuscript. Many people from many places played a role in bringing this book to publication. They are all a part of a dynamic, world-wide community of researchers, writers, and publishers.

Alexei Semenov and I still correspond via e-mail, planning new activities, conference presentations, and publications. Even though we may see each other only once a year, our friendship and collaborations continue. That's the nature of professional relationships today. I carry on meaningful dialogues with friends and colleagues around the world from my office at Montana State University. I find it all exciting and very satisfying. If you can see yourself doing the same thing, then perhaps you, too, should be a mathematician!

APPENDIX A
DIRECTORY OF STATE AGENCIES

In states with two address listings, the first address will give you information on the SSIG and Douglas programs. The second address will give information on the Byrd program.

STATE	ADDRESS
Alabama	Alabama Commission on Higher Education Suite 221, One Court Square Montgomery, AL 36197-0001 Tel: (205) 269-2700
	State Department of Education 111 Coliseum Boulevard Montgomery, AL 36193 Tel: (205) 261-2746
Alaska	Alaska Commission on Postsecondary Education Post Office Box FP Juneau, AK 99811 Tel: (907) 465-2854
	State Department of Education Post Office Box F Juneau, AK 99811 Tel: (907) 465-2841

Arizona	Arizona Commission for Postsecondary Education 3030 North Central Ave., Suite 1407 Phoenix, AZ 85012 Tel: (602) 255-3109
	State Department of Education 1535 West Jefferson Phoenix, AZ 85007 Tel: (602) 255-4770
Arkansas	Arkansas Department of Higher Education 1220 West Third Street Little Rock, AR 72201 Tel: (501) 371-1441
	Arkansas Department of Education 4 Capitol Mall Little Rock, AR 72201 Tel: (501) 371-1464
California	California Student Aid Commission 1515 S Street, North Bldg. Suite 500, P.O. Box 942845 Sacramento, CA 94245-0845 Tel: (916) 445-0880
	State Department of Education 721 Capitol Mall Sacramento, CA 95814 Tel: (916) 445-4338
Colorado	Colorado Commission on Higher Education Colorado Heritage Center 1300 Broadway, 2nd Floor Denver, CO 80203 Tel: (303) 866-2723

State Department of Education
201 East Colfax Avenue
Denver, CO 80203
Tel: (303) 866-6806

Connecticut Connecticut Department of Higher
Education
61 Woodland Street
Hartford, CT 06105-2391
Tel: (203) 566-2618

Delaware Delaware Postsecondary Education
Commission
Carvel State Office Building
820 North French Street, 4th Floor
Wilmington, DE 19801
Tel: (302) 571-3240

State Department of Public Instruction
Post Office Box 1402
Dover, DE 19903
Tel: (302) 736-4688

District of Department of Human Services
Columbia 1331 H Street NW, Suite 600
Washington, DC 20005
Tel: (202) 727-3688

District of Columbia Public Schools
415 12th Street NW
Washington, DC 20004
Tel: (202) 724-4201

Florida Florida Department of Education
Office of Student Financial Assistance
Knott Building
Tallahassee, FL 32399
Tel: (904) 488-1034

State Department of Education
Knott Building
Tallahassee, FL 32399
Tel: (904) 488-1034

Georgia   Georgia Student Finance Authority
State Loans & Grants Division
2082 East Exchange Place Suite 200
Tucker, GA 30084
Tel: (404) 493-5452

State Department of Education
Twin Towers East
Atlanta, GA 30334
Tel: (404) 656-5812

Hawaii   Hawaii State Postsecondary Education
Commission
2444 Dole Street, Room 209
Honolulu, HI 96822
Tel: (808) 948-8213

State Department of Education
Post Office Box 2360
Honolulu, HI 96804
Tel: (808) 373-2487

Idaho   Office of the State Board of Education
Len B. Jordan Building, Room 307
650 West State Street
Boise, ID 83720
Tel: (208) 334-2270

State Department of Education
650 West State Street
Boise, ID 83720
Tel: (208) 334-3300

Illinois	Illinois State Scholarship Commission
	106 Wilmot Road
	Deerfield, IL 60015
	Tel: (312) 948-8500

State Board of Education
100 North First Street
Springfield, IL 62777
Tel: (217) 782-5728

Indiana
State Student Assistance Commission of Indiana
964 North Pennsylvania Street, 1st Floor
Indianapolis, IN 46204
Tel: (317) 232-2350

State Department of Education
Room 229 — State House
Center for School Improvement &
Performance
Indianapolis, IN 46204-2798
Tel: (317) 269-9606

Iowa
Iowa College Aid Commission
201 Jewett Building
Ninth and Grand Avenue
Des Moines, IA 50309
Tel: (515) 281-3501

State Department of Education
Grimes State Office Building
Bureau of Instruction & Curriculum
Des Moines, IA 50319-0146
Tel: (515) 281-3198

Kansas
Kansas Board of Regents
Suite 609, Capitol Tower
400 West 8th Street

Topeka, KS 66603
Tel: (913) 296-3517

State Department of Education
Kansas State Education Bldg.
120 East Tenth Street
Topeka, KS 66612-1103
Tel: (913) 296-2306

Kentucky   Kentucky Higher Education Assistance
Authority
1050 U.S. 127 South
Frankfurt, KY 40601
Tel: (502) 564-4928

State Department of Education
Capital Plaza Tower
Frankfurt, KY 40601
Tel: (502) 564-4770

Louisiana   Governor's Special Commission on
Education Services
Post Office Box 44127
Baton Rouge, LA 70804
Tel: (504) 342-9422

State Department of Education
Post Office Box 44064
Bureau of Secondary Education
Baton Rouge, LA 70804-9064
Tel: (504) 342-3404

Maine   Department of Educational and Cultural
Services
Higher Education Services
State House Station #119
Augusta, ME 04333
Tel: (207) 289-2183

Maryland	Maryland State Scholarship Administration 2100 Guilford Avenue Baltimore, MD 21218 Tel: (301) 333-6450
	State Department of Education 200 West Baltimore Street Baltimore, MD 21201-2595 Tel: (301) 333-2200
Massachusetts	Board of Regents of Higher Education Scholarship Office 150 Causeway Street, Room 600 Boston, MA 02114 Tel: (617) 727-9420
	State Department of Education Quincy Center Plaza 1385 Hancock Street Quincy, MA 02169-5183 Tel: (617) 770-7300
Michigan	Michigan Department of Education Scholarship and Tuition Grant Program Post Office Box 30008 Lansing, MI 48909 Tel: (517) 373-3394
Minnesota	Minnesota Higher Education Coordinating Board 400 Capitol Square Building 500 Cedar Street St. Paul, MN 55101 Tel: (612) 296-9657
	State Department of Education 684 Capitol Square Building 550 Cedar Street

St. Paul, MN 55101
Tel: (612) 296-4067

Mississippi Mississippi Postsecondary Education
Financial Assistance Board
Post Office Box 2336
Jackson, MS 39225-2336
Tel: (601) 982-6570

State Department of Education
Post Office Box 771
Jackson, MS 39205
Tel: (601) 359-3513

Missouri Missouri Coordinating Board for Higher
Education
101 Adams Street
Jefferson City, MO 65101
Tel: (314) 751-2361

State Department of Elementary and
Secondary Education
Post Office Box 480
Jefferson City, MO 65102
Tel: (314) 751-2931

Montana Montana University System
33 South Last Chance Gulch
Helena, MT 59620
Tel: (406) 444-6570

State Office of Public Instruction
State Capitol, Room 106
Helena, MT 59620
Tel: (406) 444-3095

Nebraska Nebraska Coordinating Commission for
Postsecondary Education

Post Office Box 95005
301 Centennial Mall South
Lincoln, NE 68509
Tel: (402) 471-2847

State Department of Education
301 Centennial Mall South
Post Office Box 94987
Lincoln, NE 68509
Tel: (402) 471-2295

Nevada
State Department of Education
Capitol Complex
Carson City, NV 89710
Tel: (702) 885-5914

New
Hampshire
New Hampshire Postsecondary Education
Commission
2 1/2 Beacon Street
Concord, NH 03301
Tel: (603) 271-2555

State Department of Education
State Office Park South
101 Pleasant Street
Concord, NH 03301
Tel: (603) 271-3453

New Jersey
New Jersey Department of Higher Education
Tuition Aid Grant Program
4 Quakerbridge Plaza CN 540
Trenton, NJ 08625
Tel: (609) 588-3268

State Department of Education
225 West State Street, CN 500
Trenton, NJ 08625-0500
Tel: (609) 984-8281

New Mexico	Commission on Higher Education 1068 Cerrillos Road Santa Fe, NM 87501-4925 Tel: (505) 827-8300
	New Mexico Student Loan Guarantee Corporation Post Office Box 27020 Albuquerque, NM 87125-7020 Tel: (505) 345-3371
	State Department of Education Education Building Santa Fe, NM 87501-2786 Tel: (505) 827-6673
New York	New York State Higher Education Services Corporation One Commerce Plaza Albany, NY 12255 Tel: (518) 473-0431
	State Education Department 111 Education Building Albany, NY 12234 Tel: (518) 474-5902
North Carolina	North Carolina State Education Assistance Authority Post Office Box 2688 Chapel Hill, NC 27514 Tel: (919) 549-8614
	State Department of Public Instruction Division of Teacher Education 116 West Edenton Street Raleigh, NC 27603-1712 Tel: (919) 733-4736

North Dakota	North Dakota State Board of Higher Education Tenth Floor, State Capitol Bismarck, ND 58505-0154 Tel: (701) 224-4114
	State Department of Public Instruction State Capitol Bldg., 9th Floor Bismarck, ND 58505 Tel: (701) 224-2098
Ohio	Ohio Board of Regents 3600 State Office Tower 30 East Broad Street Columbus, OH 43299-0417 Tel: (614) 466-7420
	Ohio Student Loan Commission 50 West Broad Street Columbus, OH 43266-0504 Tel: (614) 462-6549
	State Department of Education 65 South Front Street Columbus, OH 43266-0308 Tel: (614) 466-3304
Oklahoma	Oklahoma State Regents for Higher Education 500 Education Building State Capitol Complex Oklahoma City, OK 73105 Tel: (405) 521-2444
	State Department of Education 2500 North Lincoln Boulevard Oklahoma City, OK 73105-4599 Tel: (405) 521-3301

Oregon	Oregon State Scholarship Commission 1445 Willamette Street Eugene, OR 97401 Tel: (503) 686-4166
	State Department of Education State Scholarship Commission 1445 Willamette Street #9 Eugene, OR 97401 Tel: (503) 668-4166
Pennsylvania	Pennsylvania Higher Education Assistance Authority 660 Boas Street Towne House Apartments Harrisburg, PA 17102 Tel: (717) 257-2800
	State Department of Education 333 Market Street Harrisburg, PA 17126-0333 Tel: (717) 787-3785
Rhode Island	Rhode Island Higher Education Assistance Authority 560 Jefferson Boulevard Warwick, RI 02886 Tel: (401) 277-2050
	State Department of Education 22 Hayes Street Providence, RI 02908 Tel: (401) 277-2031
South Carolina	South Carolina Higher Education Tuition Grants Agency 1310 Lady Street 411 Keenan Building

Columbia, SC 29201
Tel: (803) 734-1200

South Carolina Student Loan Corporation
Post Office Box 21487
Columbia, SC 29221
Tel: (803) 798-0916

State Department of Education
Rutledge Office Building
1429 Senate Street
Columbia, SC 29201
Tel: (803) 734-8366

South Dakota	South Dakota Department of Education and Cultural Affairs Office of the Secretary 700 Governors Drive Pierre, SD 57501-2293 Tel: (605) 773-3134
Tennessee	Tennessee Student Assistance Corporation Suite 1950, Parkway Towers 404 James Robertson Parkway Nashville, TN 37219-5097 Tel: (615) 741-1737
	State Department of Education Cordell Hull Building Nashville, TN 37219-5335 Tel: (615) 741-2731
Texas	Texas Higher Education Coordinating Board Post Office Box 12788 Capitol Station Austin, TX 78711 Tel: (512) 462-6325

Texas State Education Agency
B. Travis Building
1701 N. Congress Avenue
Austin, TX 78701-1494
Tel: (512) 463-9734

Utah   Utah State Board of Regents
Utah System of Higher Education
355 West North Temple
#3 Triad Center, Suite 550
Salt Lake City, UT 84180-1205
Tel: (801) 538-5256

Utah State Office of Education
250 East 500 South
Salt Lake City, UT 84111
Tel: (801) 538-7741

Vermont   Vermont Student Assistance Corporation
Champlain Mill
Post Office Box 2000
Winooski, VT 05404
Tel: (802) 655-9602

Virginia   State Council of Higher Education for
Virginia
James Monroe Building
101 North Fourteenth Street
Richmond, VA 23219
Tel: (804) 225-2137

State Department of Education
Post Office Box 6Q
Richmond, VA 23216-2060
Tel: (804) 225-2071

Washington	Washington State Higher Education Coordinating Board 917 Lakeridge Morris Business Park Mail Stop GV-11 Olympia, WA 98502 Tel: (206) 586-6404
	State Department of Public Instruction Division of Special Services and Professional Programs Old Capitol Building FG11 Olympia, WA 98504 Tel: (206) 586-6904
West Virginia	West Virginia Board of Regents Post Office Box 3368 950 Kanawha Boulevard East Charleston, WV 25301 Tel: (304) 348-2101
	State Department of Education 1900 Washington Street Building B, Room 358 Charleston, WV 25305 Tel: (304) 348-3691
Wisconsin	Higher Educational Aids Board 25 W. Main Street Madison, WI 53707 Tel: (608) 266-1660
	State Department of Public Instruction 125 South Webster Street Post Office Box 7841 Madison, WI 53703 Tel: (608) 266-2364

Wyoming   Wyoming Community College Commission
               2301 Central Avenue
               Barrett Building, 3rd Floor
               Cheyenne, WY 82002
               Tel: (307) 777-7763

               State Department of Education
               Hathaway Building
               Cheyenne, WY 82002
               Tel: (307) 777-7675

APPENDIX B
ORGANIZATIONS SUPPORTING
THE DEVELOPMENT OF MATH
AND SCIENCE TALENT

The following organizations offer assistance to students with an interest in mathematics, science, and engineering. They may be able to help you identify and contact potential mentors.

Society of Women Engineers
United Engineering Center
345 East 47th Street
New York, NY 10017

Bell Labs Engineering Scholarships
BLESP Administrator
150 JFK Parkway
Short Hills, NJ 07078

National Action Council for Minorities in Engineering
3 West 35th Street
New York, NY 10001

National Chicano Council on Higher Education
c/o Rafael Magallan
710 North College Ave
Claremont, CA 91711-3921

American Indian Science and Engineering Society
PO Box 606
Gettysburg, PA 17325

IBM Minority/Women Fellowships
PO Box 218
Yorktown Heights, NY 10598

Society of Actuaries
208 South La Salle Street
Chicago, IL 60604

The Mathematical Association of America
1225 Connecticut Ave NW
Washington, DC 20036

The National Council of Teachers of Mathematics (NCTM)
1906 Association Drive
Reston, VA 22091

Women and Mathematics Education (an affiliate of NCTM)
Mount Holyoke College
302 Shattuck Hall
South Hadley, MA 01075

American Mathematical Society
PO Box 6248
Providence, RI 02940

GLOSSARY

ACTUARY. A professional mathematician who uses probability and statistics to determine insurance premiums for insurance companies.

ANALYTIC GEOMETRY. Geometry from an algebraic perspective.

CARTESIAN COORDINATE SYSTEM. The system developed by Descartes for graphing functions of one and two variables. It consists of X, Y, and Z axes that intersect at their origins at right angles to each other. On each axis, positive numbers increase to the right of the origin and negative numbers decrease to the left of the origin.

CD-ROM. Compact disk information storage.

CENTER OF PROJECTION. The point from which a 3-dimensional object is projected onto a viewing plane. Point of view.

COLLINEAR. Points are collinear if they lie on the same line.

COMPLEX NUMBER. A number of the form $a + bi$, where a and b are real numbers and i is the square root of -1.

CONCURRENT. Lines are concurrent if they intersect at the same point.

CONGRUENT. Two objects are congruent if they have identical linear and angular measurements.

CONVERGENT. A sequence or series is convergent when it has a limit.

CONVEX POLYGON. A polygon with no "dents," or interior angles greater than 180 degrees.

DISTRIBUTION. The relative frequencies of occurrence of the various elements of a data set.

ELECTRONIC MAIL. Messages sent and received over computers and computer networks.

EUCLIDEAN GEOMETRY. The study of 1-, 2-, and 3-dimensional Euclidean space. First organized in Euclid's *Elements*.

EUCLIDEAN PLANE. 2-dimensional Euclidean space, usually represented as the plane $Z = 1$ in 3-space.

FINITE GRAPH. A way of representing data in which a finite set of points called vertices are joined by a finite set of line segments called edges that indicate the relationship between the vertices.

FRACTAL. An object, such as the Koch snowflake, that is composed of a curve or shape repeated on different scales.

FRIEZE. A long, horizontal decorative band.

FRIEZE PATTERN. One of seven possible patterns, each involving a different type of symmetry, that are used to create ornamental friezes.

FUNCTIONAL NOTATION. The traditional way of representing a function, or relationship, between one or more variables; variables and their coefficients are in equation form. As opposed to matrix notation, in which coefficients are arranged in rows and columns.

GRAPH THEORY. A study of finite sets of points and the relationships between them.

HALF-TURN SYMMETRY. Symmetry about a point. Applies to an object that looks the same after being rotated 180 degrees about the point.

HYPERBOLIC GEOMETRY. A geometry in which there are infinitely many parallel lines to a given line through a point not on the given line. Also called Lobachevskian geometry.

INTERNET. An international network of computer networks linking schools and scholars around the world. Used to send and receive electronic mail, satellite images, software, and so on.

ITERATED FUNCTION SYSTEM. Any system of equations that are applied in succession to a point or geometrical object.

LINE OF SYMMETRY. Divides an object into two congruent parts, each the mirror image of the other.

LINEAR TRANSFORMATION. An operation that reshapes and/or relocates objects, while preserving collinearity and concurrence. Includes translations, rotations, reflections, shears, strains, and dilations.

MAPPING. Applying a mathematical function, such as a linear transformation.

MATLAB. A computer program for doing matrix algebra.

MATRIX. An $n \times m$ rectangular array of numbers and/or variables.

MATRIX ALGEBRA. The study of matrices and their algebraic properties and applications.

MATRIX NOTATION. A way of representing a function, or relationship between one or more variables; coefficients of the variables are arranged in rows and columns. An alternative to functional notation.

MENTOR. A teacher and research supervisor.

MOTIF. A design that is repeated over and over again.

NCSA. The National Center for Supercomputing Applications.

NON-EUCLIDEAN GEOMETRY. Any geometry other than Euclid's.

NUMBER THEORY. The study of numbers and their relationships.

PERIMETER. The distance around a polygon.

POINT OF SYMMETRY. If an object has point symmetry, it looks the same after being rotated about the point 180 degrees.

PRIME NUMBER. An integer greater than 1 having no whole number divisors smaller than itself, other than 1.

PROBABILITY. The study of the chance or likelihood associated with various events.

PROJECTIVE GEOMETRY. The study of perspective relationships between various objects.

ROTATION. A linear transformation that preserves the size and shape of an object while turning it about some center.

SCIENTIFIC VISUALIZATION. The science and art of representing data sets as images.

SHEAR. A linear transformation similar to the distortion achieved when a deck of cards is shoved to the side while leaving the bottom card in place.

SIMILAR. Two objects are similar if one has the same proportions as the other.

SIMPLEX. A convex geometrical form in three or more dimensions. In three dimensions, it is formed by connecting four vertices on the surface of a sphere.

STATISTICS. The representation, analysis, and interpretation of sample data.

STRAIN. A stretch or compression along one axis.

STRANGE ATTRACTOR. The fractal object generated by an iterated function system of contractive linear transformations.

SYSTEM OF EQUATIONS. Two or more algebraic equations that together represent some set of conditions.

TILE THE PLANE. To cover a plane with objects that do not overlap or leave gaps.

TRANSLATION. A linear translation that slides an object from one location to another while maintaining its orientation.

SOURCES

CHAPTER 1

Krantz, Les, ed. *Jobs Rated Almanac Two*. Mahwah, N.J.: World Almanac, 1992.

Working Groups of the Commission on Standards for School Mathematics of the National Council of Teachers of Mathematics. *Curriculum and Evaluation Standards for School Mathematics*. Reston, Va.: NCTM, 1989.

CHAPTER 2

Science Service, 1719 N Street NW, Washington, DC 20036.

CHAPTER 3

Barnsley, Michael. *Fractals Everywhere*. San Diego, Calif.: Academic Press, Inc., 1988.

Chaos: The Software. Sausalito, Calif.: Autodesk, Inc.

The Desktop Fractal Design System. San Diego, Calif.: Academic Press, Inc., 1989.

Martin, George E. *Transformation Geometry: An Introduction to Symmetry*. New York: Springer-Verlag, 1982.

Working Groups of the Commission on Standards for School
Mathematics. *Curriculum and Evaluation Standards for
School Mathematics*. Reston, Va.: National Council of
Teachers of Mathematics, 1989.

CHAPTER 4

Hill, David R. *Experiments in Computational Matrix Algebra*.
New York: Random House, 1988.

Kastner, Bernice. *Space Mathematics*. Washington, D.C.:
NASA, 1985.

Moler, Cleve B. *MATLAB*. Available from Public Brand Software,
P.O. Box 51315, Indianapolis, IN 46251, 1984.

PC-MATLAB. The MathWorks, Inc., Suite 250, 20 North Main
St., Sherborn, MA 01770, (617)-653-1415.

PEANUT Software, Phillips Exeter Academy, Exeter, NH 03833.

Rorres, Chris, and Howard Anton. *Applications of Linear
Algebra*. New York: John Wiley & Sons, 1977.

CHAPTER 5

Cederberg, Judith N. *A Course in Modern Geometries*. New
York: Springer-Verlag, 1989.

Woodward, Ernest. "Geometry with a MIRA." In Jane M. Hill,
ed. *Geometry for Grades K-6*. Reston, Va.: NCTM, 1987.

CHAPTER 6

Rogers, David A., and J. Alan Adams. *Mathematical Elements
for Computer Graphics*, 2nd edition. New York: McGraw-
Hill Publishing Co., 1990.

CHAPTER 7

Croft, Hallard T., Kenneth J. Falconer, and Richard K. Guy.
Unsolved Problems in Geometry. New York: Springer-
Verlag, 1991.

Mandelbrot, Benoit. *The Fractal Geometry of Nature*. San
Francisco: W. H. Freeman, 1982.

Thomas, David A. *Teenagers, Teachers, and Mathematics*.
Boston: Allyn and Bacon, 1992.

Peitgen, H. O. and P. H. Richter. *The Beauty of Fractals*. New York: Springer-Verlag, 1986.

Yaglom. I. M. *Geometric Transformations*. Vols. 1–3. Washington, D.C.: Mathematical Association of America, 1979.

CHAPTER 8

National Center for Supercomputing Applications (NCSA), 605 E. Springfield Ave., University of Illinois at Urbana-Champaign, Champaign, IL 61820-5518.

Public (Software) Library, P.O. Box 35705, Houston, TX 77235-5705.

CHAPTER 9

Bicknell, M., and J. E. Hoggatt, eds. *Fibonacci's Problem Book*. San Jose, Calif.: San Jose University, Fibonacci Association, 1974.

Guy, Richard K. *Unsolved Problems in Number Theory*. New York: Springer-Verlag, 1981.

Hardy, G. H. and E. M. Wright. *Introduction to the Theory of Numbers*. Oxford: Oxford University Press, 1980.

Hoggatt, V. E. *Fibonacci and Lucas Numbers*. Boston: Houghton Mifflin, 1969.

Huntley, H. E. *The Divine Proportion*. New York: Dover, 1970.

INDEX